STORIES ABOUT STRANGERS

Swedish Media Constructions of Socio-Cultural Risk

Bo Petersson

University Press of America,® Inc.
Lanham · Boulder · New York · Toronto · Oxford

Copyright © 2006 by
University Press of America,® Inc.
4501 Forbes Boulevard
Suite 200
Lanham, Maryland 20706
UPA Acquisitions Department (301) 459-3366

PO Box 317
Oxford
OX2 9RU, UK

Library of Congress Control Number: 2006923923
ISBN-13: 978-0-7618-3508-0 (paperback : alk. paper)
ISBN-10: 0-7618-3508-3 (paperback : alk. paper)

Contents

Preface

This book has been in the making for several years. It sums up, synthesises and collects several strands of writing and argument that I have presented over the last few years. Consequently, preliminary drafts roughly corresponding to different parts of some chapters have already been published elsewhere. Very early versions of Chapters 3 and 5 have appeared in *International Journal of Peace Studies* 8:1, Spring 2003, and in the volume Bo Petersson and Eric Clark (eds): *Identity Dynamics and the Construction of Boundaries*, Lund: Nordic Academic Press (2003). A preliminary version of the arguments made in Chapter 4, as well as some central findings reported on in Chapter 6, were published in Karin Borevi and Per Strömblad (eds): *Kategorisering och integration. Om föreställda identiteter i politik, forskning, media och vardag*, Stockholm: SOU 2004:48, as well as made available online in *KBM:s temaserie* 2004:2. Those two pieces were both co-authored in Swedish with Anders Hellström. Finally, other preliminary findings included in Chapter 6 were published in Hans Brinks, Stella Rock & Edward Timms (eds): *Nationalist Myths and Modern Media*, London: I. B. Tauris (2006). I gratefully acknowledge the permission to reuse the material from all the aforementioned publications.

There would have been no book at all without the generous support from my financial sponsors: the Swedish Crisis Management Authority, the Jenz and Carl Olof Hamrin Foundation and Lund University. I hereby express my indebtedness to these institutions for making the study possible. I also thankfully acknowledge a travel grant from the Crafoord Foundation.

Any writer, not least of academic literature, can testify what a truly lonely race it is that an author embarks upon. Once in a while, however, one is fortunate enough to have discussions with friends and colleagues that make the journey less arduous, indeed worthwhile. They also—most definitely—contribute to making the emerging book decidedly better than it otherwise would have been. Several people have given generously of their time in connection with this enterprise.

First of all, I would like to extend my gratitude to Anders Hellström, who from the outset acted as my chief travelling companion in the general research project, of which this study was a part. His views and comments on drafts at different stages of completion have been most crucial. My friends and colleagues at the Department of Political Science at Lund University, Björn Badersten, Maximilian Conrad, Christian Fernández, Martin Hall, Ulrika Jerre, Sara Kalm, Catarina Kinnvall, Dalia Mukhtar-Landgren, Tom Nilsson, Sarah Scuzzarello, Ylva Stubbergaard and Anders Uhlin have likewise read and commented on what at different times has represented the complete text, an invaluable help and assistance for which I am truly grateful. Inger Sjunnesson, a rock as always, also gave me her much appreciated comments on the text in its entirety. Bo Bengtsson, Anders Blixt, Kristina Boréus, Karin Borevi, Ylva Brune, Inbal E. Cicurel, Eric Clark, Ulf Hedetoft, Volodymyr Kulyk, David May, Ulf Mörkenstam, Catharina Raudvere, Anne Julie Semb, Per Strömblad, Ray Taras, Barbara Törnquist-Plewa, Katharine Tyler, Lotta Wagnsson and Anders Wigerfelt have all provided helpful and constructive criticism on drafts or oral presentations at various stages during the process. Håkan Magnusson and Leif Johansson played essential roles in the early phases of designing the project as such. I also extend my gratitude to Annika Hughes, who not only copyedited the text and made my English more readable, but also made insightful comments on the evolving text; to Martin Sjunnesson, who made the pages camera-ready before printing; and to Adam von Seth, who prepared the index.

Having said all of this, my final words go to those closest to my heart: my dear family, Sanja, Teodor and Isidor. You give meaning to my life. Without you I would certainly have been able to find a lot more time to write this book, but I would never have been able to muster the energy to transform that spare time into anything meaningful. Teodor and Isidor: the future belongs to you. It is my heartfelt hope that you will grow up to live in an increasingly embracing and welcoming world, where stereotyped thinking about strangers has relaxed its hold. With love and affection I dedicate the book to you.

Furulund and Lund, Sweden, early February 2006

Bo Petersson

1. Introducing the Study

This study deals with the majority populations of small-town communities and their views and prejudices about immigrants. This is a topical issue. Not that migration is a novel phenomenon. It certainly is not, and there is a long history of immigration in the Western world to prove it. However, for many individuals, the arrival of immigrants of different nationalities, not previously associated with their particular community is still frequently seen as a new and threatening feature. Ingrained majority habits and traditions are often seen to be challenged in the process, which frequently leads to reactions on both sides.

In order to analyse such majority-minority encounters, I will use insights from several strands of literature, most prominently on perceptions of socio-cultural risk; stereotype-formation, scapegoating and enemy images; mass media reporting on immigrants; and the study of everyday practices, or quite simply, the mundane. These sub-fields of study are all closely related but have rarely, if ever, been brought together in previous research. In the following chapters I hope to demonstrate that this combination of perspectives is a fruitful one that enhances the understanding of majority-minority relations in contemporary Western societies. Having provided this background, there are now some more specific statements that need to be made about the principal points of departure of this book.

Firstly, one important focus is thus on the ways in which socio-cultural risk is perceived, constructed and narrated and the potential consequences that may arise from these processes. It is true that, in their everyday lives, people confront a multitude of risks (Beck 1992; Giddens 1999), and I will certainly not venture to deal with the full spectrum of these here. Instead, I will dwell on the risks and risk perceptions that are ascribed to influences believed to be strange and foreign, and thus also seen to be threatening to accustomed ways and modes of existence. These unfamiliar influences are pegged to real-life persons with real-life faces. In the cases studied in this book they are related to immigrants.

Secondly, throughout the book, another consistent argument will be that people, in order to deal with their everyday risk perceptions, communicate with their peers about them. Thus, they tell stories about what they have seen and heard, including what they have perceived as deviant and strange. Through these stories, they define what they consider to be normal according to the yardsticks that they apply and, consequently, also indicate who and what is *not* considered to be normal and why they believe this to be the case. The stories that people tell about deviations from the norm will contain a fair amount of stereotyped thinking. They will feature images of immigrant Others as feared, shunned, excluded or marginalised, or indeed all of these. Sometimes they will go so far as to nurture enemy and scapegoat images. Regardless of their shape, however, the practical consequence of this negatively stereotyped thinking will be to reinforce pre-existing discriminatory structures.

Thirdly, another central point of departure is that the people who share, tell and retell such stories about the strange are most often ordinary people, who would most certainly detest the notion of expressing thoughts or sentiments that could be seen as xenophobic or racist. Still, that is often what these sentiments are, at least with regard to their net effects. For while they may not be intentionally discriminatory, they are without a doubt excluding and marginalising in their cumulative structural impact. I will have reasons to reiterate this many times in the book, but suffice to say at this stage that the ordinary and the mundane matter, and they matter significantly.

Finally, the empirical chapters of the book will address certain named small-town communities in my native Sweden. More specifically, they deal with the adjacent municipalities of Ljungby, Markaryd and Älmhult, situated in the southern part of the country. The local discourses of the three towns will primarily be analysed as reflected through their local daily newspaper, *Smålänningen*. The towns are all inhabited by ordinary men and women, who generally would not wish harm on anyone. I am not interested in the business of naming and shaming these communities; that is a business that is as far from the priorities of my book as one could get. It is therefore imperative to stress already here that the negative stereotypes about the immigrated Others that are peddled in these small-town milieus did not come into existence there. Rather, they can be found everywhere in the Western world. Indeed, they constitute a depressingly universal phenomenon, even though the stigmatised categories and groups of people vary, depending on where in the world one studies them.

Stereotypes That We Live By

It was in the late 1970s that Edward Said (1978) published his groundbreaking book, highlighting the stereotyped images of Orientalism that were already then so prevalent and entrenched in the cultural world of the educated West, the Occident. These images, depicting a rational, illuminated, strong, able and masculine West, have continuously and consistently been contrasted with the mystical, bizarre, weak, feminised and exotic Orient. Other writers, such as Stuart Hall (1997), have since expanded our insights into the ingrained Western stereotyping structures and representations that refer to the former Western colonies and their inhabitants as subaltern, less developed, immature and often exotic entities that need to be protected, checked and taken care of by the allegedly supreme West. In the continual process of sharing, communicating and essentialising these representations, the social world is constructed accordingly. The West retains its power positions across the board and the Orient and its representatives are further marginalised.

Recent years have added another facet to the development of stereotyped images of the Orient. Since the terrorist attacks in New York City in 2001 and later in Madrid, London and elsewhere, the exotic and unfettered East has increasingly taken on the features of an essentially threatening and hostile entity who, through its representatives, seeks to bring mayhem and destruction to the privileged West. The generally projected image is thus becoming increasingly complex; the Orient Other is no longer predominantly feminised and weak, for although s/he is still erratic, s/he is also purposefully plotting to destroy the West, taking on the features of an ultra-religious and violent (Muslim) fanatic.

For the sake of clarity, it should be stressed that examples of the latter, more extreme strands of reasoning have barely been notable at all in the local discourses that I have studied for the purposes of this book. But the general background that they form has most certainly added to the general feelings of uncertainty that underpin and prompt adversity to strangers in local settings. For while people may rarely fear terrorist attacks in their tranquil small-town environments, they are certainly aware of what happens in the world at large. Local milieus are not isolated from national and global contexts, even though they constitute a less exposed part of them. TV reports reach the living rooms of most people, regardless of whether they live in London or Ljungby, Basingstoke or Berlin.

Opinions that draw on the stereotyped images of the Other as strange, erratic and counter to Western norms are nourished and reinforced in numerous ways—in upbringing, in education, in the mass media, and in everyday discourse. Indeed, in the Western world, they have been with us for hundreds of years already and they are certainly not easy to change, let alone rock or dispel. Ideas about the supremacy of the West are so tenacious that, even in the light of seemingly overwhelming counterevidence, they are most likely to remain with us for several generations yet. It would thus be more than unfair and unjustified to single out any particular communities as being especially bad culprits when it comes to clinging to negative and stereotyped images of immigrated Others. Quite on the contrary, they merely represent sentiments that are present universally in, at the very least, all Western societies (van Dijk 1987). Thus, the milieus that I have selected for this study just happen to give concrete frames and backgrounds to the invocation of certain familiar stereotypes and negative ideas and representations of perceived strangers. It could be argued that the naming of individual places in itself implies a certain amount of finger-pointing. However, making references to concrete places and faces is, I believe, necessary in order to get the message across that these racialised ideas and representations constitute not only a very real but also a highly salient social phenomenon in the here and now, in many sites, indeed everywhere. And although the images are socially constructed, they do have depressingly real consequences for immigrated people. For this reason, if we spread awareness of them, we may be able to mitigate their consequences, at least to some degree. This might be a vain hope, but it constitutes the very rationale behind this book.

Even in Sweden

I am a Swedish-born scholar representing Swedish academic life. There is no denying that this has been a pivotal reason for the choice of the empirical cases dealt with in this book. However, in view of the universality of the phenomenon of stereotyping and excluding strangers, there are also more substantial grounds for choosing Swedish cases specifically. Throughout most of the post-war period, Sweden was widely, at home and abroad, depicted as a, maybe even *the*, success story of the West. The celebrated so-called 'Swedish model' served as a showcase of a true people's home, where the state, through its extensive socio-economic safety net, catered for everybody's needs, from the cradle to the grave. In this imagery, Sweden was close to a social paradise on Earth, and if harmony and understanding between individuals and groups of people prevailed anywhere in the Western world, this was it. During the past 15 years or so, however, this picture has gradually started to change. In the early 1990s, a newly established populist party, New Democracy, made it to the Swedish parliament, carried to electoral success by a largely xenophobic agenda. Although the party's existence was to be short-lived in the parliamentary arena (it crashed in the next general elections and was dissolved soon thereafter), it contributed to the setting of a harsher tone against immigrants in the public Swedish debate, as well as in popular discourse at large.

During the 1960s and 1970s, when the Swedish model was still in its heyday and the Swedish economy boomed, migrants from abroad were on the whole cordially welcomed to fill vacancies in the labour market. From the 1980s and, above all, the 1990s onwards, there was a change in the socio-economic climate, from a fair-weather prognosis to a stormier one. During these years, there was a shift in the overall composition of migrants to Sweden, from migrant workers to people who were prompted by other reasons, such as the need to seek political refuge from persecution and widespread destruction, not least in connection with the Balkan wars. The Swedish societal climate became increasingly frosty and forbidding towards immigrants. The most visible sign of this was the aforementioned establishment of New Democracy and the simultaneous increase in the activities of progressively more assertive xenophobic and extremist fringe forces on the ultra right, even though the latter were scattered and comparatively devoid of influence.

Despite all this, however, abroad there was a surprising tenacity to the old image of Sweden as a model country of well-being and harmony. The Swedish model still held its sway as an international trademark, even if it, to all appearances, had outlived itself in Sweden (cf. for example discussions in Russia as reported in Petersson 2001:109-110). These cracks in the idyll, along with the proclamation that, even in Sweden, sentiments of racism and xenophobia had reached deep down into mainstream society, constituted the point of departure for Allan Pred's (2000) artful and celebrated book about contemporary Sweden. His line of reasoning was that, if there were visible and widespread tendencies of racism and xenophobia even in a social model country such as Sweden, it could safely be assumed that this was a phenomenon that could be encountered anywhere in the Western world. I concur with this line and I believe that it is still valid. This argument thus constitutes the final reason behind my choice of illustrative cases.

The Whys and Hows of This Book

Any writer can testify that somewhere in the process of writing a book, the text starts to lead its own existence. The manuscript that has been so carefully planned by the author, slowly but deliberately starts to develop in other directions than was originally intended. This book is no exception to this rule. On beginning the project, I actually set out to write The Ljungby Story, the aim of which was to recount, through the prism of the predominant local newspaper, what took place in Ljungby, a Swedish small-town community, during one single year, with special attention given to majority-minority relations. I also had the intention to study local identity construction in general and the encounters between localism and nationalism. Above all, I was interested in studying, as closely as possible, the fabric of mundane, everyday events, and the inherent obstacles to integration into the host society that could be discerned therein, as this is what constitutes the main concern for most immigrants. Indeed, it was the seeming banality of events that was the very reason that I chose to focus on Ljungby in the first place. The town quite simply constituted a community which rarely made it into national headline news and where there were no, nationally at least, known tensions between immigrants and native Swedes. In analysing sentiments among the resident population, I was seeking local counterparts to what Michael Billig (1995) has so fittingly labelled banal nationalism, or banal localism if you will. I proceeded from the notion that such non-dramatic but nonetheless excluding structures of thought could make it difficult for foreigners to become accepted in their new communities.

Ideas about the importance of the mundane also account for the choice of the year of 2002 as my period of analysis. I wanted to analyse non-dramatic, local events during a full year, from New Year's Day through to New Year's Eve, through the prism of a local newspaper. The year was randomly selected but was above all a year when nothing exceptional happened in the town of Ljungby itself, apart from the general elections in September which, as is the tradition in

Sweden, took place on national, regional and local levels simultaneously. Thus, it was the mundane events, during a mundane year, in a mundane community in Sweden that were to provide the preconditions for the study of attitudinal obstacles to the everyday integration of immigrants into their resident society.

The attentive following of developments in a small-town community, through its local newspaper during the course of a year, could be said to place this part of the study squarely within the domain of community studies, scrutinising the prevalent modes of exclusion of marginalised groups. Although most previous studies in this field have rested on a methodology of interviews with community-members, or participant observation (Elias & Scotson 1999; Tyler 2003; Norman 2004), this book looks instead at the contents of local media outlets. First of all I set out to analyse events in Ljungby mainly through its all-pervasive local newspaper, *Smålänningen*. On the basis of my day-to-day scrutiny of the paper, I then proceeded to conduct interviews with persons that had played central roles in the enactment of majority-minority relations in the community during the year. These interviews allowed me to dig deeper beneath the surface of the social reality reported by the newspaper. I undertook two rounds of interviews, the first one together with my associate Anders Hellström, who worked with similar problems regarding other European countries (Petersson & Hellström 2004; Hellström 2006), and the second round on my own.

Ljungby was thus my primary choice of research object. The two nearby municipalities that are also featured in this book, Markaryd and Älmhult, instead rather forced themselves on me as I studied the local newspaper. For it was at this point that the text started to live its own life, as these two communities assertively suggested themselves to be more than just side-tracked settings for the overall plot. And so, in the end, The Ljungby Story became but one story among several others to be recounted in this study, as Markaryd and Älmhult superimposed themselves onto my initial ideas. That said, it remains a highly interesting and relevant story, even if, or rather just because, it tells the tale of mundane and everyday matters.

During the course of my study, however, I found that the settings of Markaryd and Älmhult in many ways offered more fertile grounds for the analysis of important subjects such as stereotyping and scapegoating, risk discourse as well as constructed and mediated stories about risk involving immigrants. These dimensions were decidedly more salient there than they were in Ljungby. Both the Älmhult and—above all—the Markaryd case clearly illustrate the fruitfulness of combining insights from research on socio-cultural risk with an analysis of stereotyping and scapegoat-formation. The two cases vividly demonstrate the premature closure and ungenerous rigidity of these processes and provide rich foundations for the analysis of how seemingly innocent and vague discourses on risk can tip over into more ominous ones of threat and imminent danger to major societal values. The Markaryd and Älmhult studies thus offer insights that are valuable for an enhanced understanding of the dynamics of majority-minority encounters. In other words, the combination and comparison of those two cases with the more mundane day-to-day rhythm exemplified by Ljungby have proved very useful for the study of the general problem of relations between resident majorities and immigrants.

The Shape of the Chapters to Come

After this introductory chapter, the remaining chapters of the book are structured as follows. Chapter 2 introduces and discusses the concept of socio-cultural risk as it has been used in the scholarly literature. It relates the term 'risk' to the closely correlated ones 'danger' and 'threat'. Furthermore, the chapter examines in more general terms how immigrants and strangers are seen to be 'risky' by resident majorities, not least in the context of globalisation, which is also considered since it brings a new sense of urgency to many encounters between majorities and minorities. In conjunction with this, there is also a brief discussion on multiculturalism and how this phenomenon may be perceived by majority groups to be the most apparent manifestation of globalisation. Last, but not least, there is an overview of previous community study literature on majority-minority relations in rural or small-town settings.

In Chapter 3, I elaborate on how stereotypes and related ideas about strangers can be seen and analysed as *stories*, or narratives, and how these can fruitfully be assessed in relation to the concept of risk. The chapter then goes on to discuss stereotypes together with concepts such as scapegoating and enemy images. It suggests how scapegoating processes may engender preventive action and outbreaks of violence and provides an empirical illustration of this. In order to underline the universality of the phenomena under discussion, this example is brought in from quite another context and milieu, telling the story of racialised riots in Moscow in the first years of the 21st century and of their background in the conflict-ridden and stereotype-infested tension between Russians and Chechens. This case illustrates how far out of hand matters actually can get and what additional impact enemy images and scapegoating phenomena may have in already tense and confrontational settings.

In Chapter 4, the fundamental role of the mass media in the construction of everyday existence is discussed. The importance of studying everyday practices is explained and underlined, as well as the pivotal role of mass media in this regard. Also, the chapter discusses the role of, primarily, local news media for the shaping and moulding of readers' perceptions of the world around them. A discussion is undertaken on why the media should be seen as a societal actor, as well as an arena for debate and action. In relation to this, there is an overview of the kinds of stereotypical media images about immigrants that have been identified in earlier research. In general terms, immigrants have been prone to be associated with threat, criminality, illness, uncleanliness and liabilities in general. In order to underline once again the universality of these societal phenomena, some empirical examples are taken from the Danish socio-political scene. Above all, a story is recounted about refugee children at a municipal preschool who, due to diagnosed illness, were depicted as posing major threats to 'Danish' children in the local community. This illustration ends the chapter.

Chapter 5 is the first empirical chapter of the study. It underlines the resilience of stereotypes and the latency of scapegoating phenomena. The chapter centres on sentiments of assertive rather than banal localism, manifesting itself in the exclusionary practices and open xenophobia found among representatives of the majority population in the small Swedish town of Markaryd. The way in which the story unfolded made it clear that the episode was drastic by Swedish standards. In contrast to the following two empirical chapters, here there had already been a departure from the mundane, the localism was not so banal anymore and the societal risk discourse had evolved into a discourse of imminent danger. The major story in the chapter concerns local reactions to a perceived increase in minor crime, which was attributed to the arrival of large numbers of asylum-seekers to the municipality. As a response from the resident majority, vigilante groups started to form and there was an evident and threatening polarisation between Us and Them. Through its reporting, the local newspaper articulated and reinforced existing stereotypes about the asylum-seekers. Different strands of argumentation were followed as to why the immigrated groups in question should be regarded as alien to the community at large. The chapter ends with an attempt to offer some background factors regarding why the situation became so bad precisely in Markaryd.

In Chapter 6, the focus shifts back to what, from the outset, was the main setting of the book, namely the small-town of Ljungby. The mundane, in other words, re-emerges. The main focus of this chapter is to give an account of the non-dramatic events that took place in the town during a typical year in the early 21st century—2002—how these were reflected upon in the local newspaper, what roles immigrants were attributed in these stories, and what this indicates about the hold that stereotypical thinking about foreigners had on the majority population. In order to illustrate the tenacity of stereotypes, and to further bring home the point that stereotypical images are not only widespread in a spatial sense but also travel fairly intact across time (Mörkenstam 2004), the chapter begins with a foray into the Ljungby of the late 1980s, as it was reported on by the local newspaper. As before, the chosen year—1987—was largely randomly selected, the rationale being to provide a point of reference with which it would be possible to make comparisons over time. More specifically, this year represented a period when strangers were a far rarer phenomenon in Ljungby, as well as an era in which the Berlin Wall still stood tall and the word 'globalisation' had not yet become a buzzword in Sweden or, for that matter, in the rest of the Western world. This provides an insight into the continuity of certain stereotypes and ideas about socio-cultural risk, at the same time as it is also evident that important changes have taken place in the town. Just as intended, Chapter 6 deals throughout with rather pedestrian texts, collected from the local newspaper, which most of the time tell the readers little that is out of the ordinary. Attention is again given to how the local paper articulates and reinforces stereotypes about immigrated groups. There is a special focus on reports that depict immigrants and refugees either as perpetrators or as victims—or, occasionally, as relatively successful people cast in the role of the few exceptions that prove the rule. A major conclusion of the chapter is that immigrants are absent from the reports on everyday situations that local newspapers otherwise excel in writing, and that this amounts to a serious obstacle to integration into the ways and mores of the majority society.

In Chapter 7, there is a short and bizarre but nonetheless revealing story about the kinds of prejudice prevalent in the perception of strangers in the local community of Älmhult. This is a small-town which, as the cradle of the internationally renowned furniture store IKEA, would otherwise be expected to be more open to global influences. More specifically, the chapter deals with two partly contrasting cases that together illuminate how images of strangers are constructed in this local setting. Curiously, both cases involve local pizzerias and it is shown how these restaurants are depicted as a location of the strange and risky. There are xenophobic as well as racialised and gendered undercurrents to the stories. Both pizzeria cases deal with so-called urban legends that involve stereotyping and rumours and they bear out the key role of news media in giving credence and status to rumours that are spread locally.

In Chapter 8, I turn to the conclusion of the book. The main arguments are summarised and I address the more principal issues that have been raised during the course of the study. I also venture to advance some ideas on how to combat the phenomena of prejudicial thinking and negative stereotyping in contemporary societies in the Western world. As stated above, this is the ultimate motive behind the book.

2. Constructions of Socio-Cultural Risk

The subject of risk has gained increasing attention over recent years, as scholarly arguments about risk and risk-related areas have multiplied. As one commentator put it, the concept 'is an idiom so infused with self-evident importance that few dare question its utility' (Jarvis 2004:305). Risk is by definition a bad thing which, according to plain common sense, has to be countered. The popularity of the concept might entail some undesired consequences; phenomena previously referred to by other terms have now become squeezed in under the risk rubric. As the commentator dryly remarked, risk seems to be 'the best thing discovered since sliced bread' (Jarvis 2004:305). This is the problem with popular concepts; they tend to take over even when this is unwarranted and hence become overstretched. This work builds, however, on understandings of risk that have been elaborated on in scholarly literature during the previous two decades at least. Thus, the overstretch can hopefully be at least alleviated.

Addressing Risk

The risk concept as connected to societal factors and more indeterminate sources of risk has been dealt with in the intellectual traditions of three major theoretical approaches (Lupton 1999:1-11): the cultural and symbolic one following the writings of Mary Douglas (1985, 1992), the risk society tradition as represented by sociologists Ulrich Beck (1992) and Anthony Giddens (1999), and the 'governmentality' tradition of Michel Foucault (1991). Whereas the risk society tradition provides numerous insights regarding macro structures of contemporary post-modern society, it has little to offer with regard to the dynamics that risk society invites and ushers in at the micro level, in ordinary peoples' everyday activities.

The governmentality perspective gives a major contribution to risk analysis through its focus on elite linguistic constructions and how populations through these means are checked within prescribed parameters of normality. Still, the exclusionary dynamics as practiced on the ground are to my mind best accounted for in the tradition associated with the anthropologist Mary Douglas. Deborah Lupton (1999:6) argues in an overview that all three approaches rarely tend to leave the ivory towers of grand theory to deal with empirical studies 'into the ways in which people conceptualize and experience risk as part of their daily lives', but I do not concur here. Academic writing following Mary Douglas' cultural and symbolic tradition lends itself well to empirical work. In the chapters to come I shall try to demonstrate that this is the case.

For Mary Douglas and her followers, the point of departure is that ideas of purity and contamination serve as basic building blocks for notions about where and how to draw cultural boundaries between the included Us and the excluded Them. Those individuals and groups who by majority norms are not deemed to be fully 'normal' are considered risky; they pose, albeit vague and diffuse, risks to themselves, to the members of the majority and to society at large. Importantly, perceptions of risks are per se instrumental in upholding the symbolic boundaries within a community (Tulloch & Lupton 2003:6). The risky groups are regarded as Other, whereas the non-risky 'normal' groups constitute the collective Self which endeavours to avoid risk. Certainly, the 'normal' groups have great prospects to do so, as they are the wielders of the norms of truth; they just have to live by their own rules (Young 2000).

Following Beck's understanding (1992), risk has been part of human existence ever since the onset of modernisation. In our contemporary times, this has become more accentuated than ever. Environmental hazards stemming from industrial emissions of toxic waste, for instance, constitute one major risk to be encountered. However, Beck argues that such, essentially man-made, risks have become endemic to our existence in the sense that we know that they are there, but we have learned to live with them and they do not really affect our daily lives. There is an awareness of a multitude of potentially pressing problems, but low probability is attributed to scenarios where these problems materialise. This is in contrast to the vocabulary on threats which signals urgency, priority and high probability of undesired outcomes (Stripple 2005).

Indeed, 'threat' is a concept which is highly related to the concept of risk. The same goes for 'danger'. Yet, these concepts all have slightly different connotations. In one of her essays, Mary Douglas (1992:24-25) seems to tacitly deplore the fact that 'risk' and 'danger' have acquired the status of synonyms in everyday discourse. I can see the merits of trying to keep these related concepts apart. In my view, notions of risk and threat are both about danger, and what differentiates them is whether or not these notions are fraught with uncertainty. Both categories contain ideas about something bad that might harm us, our nearest and dearest, our material belongings or the values and traditions that we cherish. The difference between 'risk' and 'threat' lies in the language that is employed and the attributes that are given to the projected outcomes: urgency, priority and high probability in the case of threat, and latency, unclear priorities and hence low probability in the case of risk[1]. Or, put somewhat differently, when risk is projected, uncertainty reigns, and stories are told about dangers that *might* materialise. In the case of threat, however, the assessments are made with certainty; the bad things are said to be here already.

The reader should note that I am discussing perceptions here and that I thus employ the logic that if something is *perceived* by a person as a threat, then it also *is* a threat to him/her. Thus, the debate about whether these threats are 'real' or not, whether they are 'objectively there' or not, is actually beside the point. This is not of course to deny the materiality, as well as the realness of a depressingly large number of horrific and frightening phenomena in today's world (cf. Douglas 1992:29). Neither is it to deny that there are likewise several phenomena out there where it seems much less justified to talk about 'real grounds' for fear, nor where the alleged dangers at any rate would strike an outside observer as grossly exaggerated. Let me thus repeat that when people perceive something as risky or threatening it is for all practical purposes risky and threatening for them, at least in the context in which they address the subject. Whether the risk or threat is 'really' there or not is not actually relevant when one tries to discern the perceptions employed. And when these are in focus, as they are in the present study, 'objective' risk is not a sufficient explanation for perceived risk (Sjöberg & Engelberg 2005:328).

Thus, if estimates about danger are uncertain and vague, they do not signal urgency. Instead, the projected danger is said to be latent and the assessments convey a story about something that might go wrong or harm us in a fairly distant future. In such cases, there are estimations of risk. If, on the other hand, there are estimates to the effect that the danger is already here, that something bad has indeed already befallen us or is at the very point of doing so, then there has already been a departure from a discourse of risk. Speedy action of a preemptory kind is often a logical recommendation emanating from this kind of language. In these cases, it is more to the point to refer to estimations of threat.

However, even if one makes these delimitations in relation to neighbouring concepts, the concept of risk remains broad and encompassing. In view of the overextension of the concept, there is still a need to narrow down the domain. Moreover, when the parameters of risk are restricted to merely encompass nonalarmist perceptions of what might go wrong under unfortunate circumstances, the area is still so broad that it is analytically less than helpful for scholarly analysis. Let us therefore return to the subject of socio-cultural risk.

Discussing Socio-Cultural Risk

If we hold on to the concept of risk as inspired by Beck a little longer, we find that risk discourse in this tradition is often clad in rational garb. It is technical and calculating, whereas the discourse on threats is much more emotional and highly-strung: the ills are here now, and we must take action at once, or else disaster will strike us (cf. Stripple 2005).

There is a notable difference here compared with the Mary Douglas tradition of cultural and symbolic risk. The discourse that will be analysed in the following chapters is indeed both emotional and highly-strung. Yet, what is under discussion is most of the time undeniably connected with risk, not with threat. Other elements of the differentiations made above still hold, however. There is a vagueness and indeterminacy inherent in the examples of discussions on socio-cultural risk that we will encounter. Most of them cannot be said to be pursued because of the detection of an imminent and present social ill; rumours instead, for instance, play an important part. There is however one useful differentiation that one can make here on the basis of the distinctions proposed within the Beck tradition. In cases where socio-cultural risk discourse starts to change into a discourse on threat, conditions begin to ripen for preventative action. This is something to look out for. We need to know more about the dynamics involved when a risk discourse starts to evolve into one of threat, since this is where highly detrimental consequences may ensue. More bluntly put, this is where people may actually start to physically harm each other.

It is a central point of departure in this book that risk discourses about immigrants among majority populations are negative and undesired phenomena, as they signal prejudice and less than embracing attitudes to strangers. However, it is when the sceptical but comparatively non-alarmist risk discourse evolves into one of clearly articulated threat that tangible and harmful societal effects are likely to follow. Majority populations may become convinced that formidable threats do or will soon emanate from the immigrants and that these threats therefore need to be nipped in their buds. This changeover is tantamount to the transition from banal, everyday nationalism into a hot and conflict-seeking one (cf. Billig 1995). The seemingly harmless variants of attitudinal phenomena need to be researched into, for it is they that provide the preconditions, as well as the cognitive and emotive underpinnings that their hot counterparts thrive upon.

Risk perceptions are made at an individual level but can in several respects be seen as collective phenomena. In Parekh's (2000:143) understanding of culture, which I find useful here, culture is a 'historically created system of meaning and significance' or a 'system of beliefs and practices in terms of which a group of human beings understand, regulate and structure their individual and collective lives'. It is one of my fundamental arguments that perceptions about societal risks are socially constructed and culturally shared. As I will endeavour to show, they are prevalent in, among other things, prejudicial structures, stereotypes and negative images about the Other. Such sentiments and ideas are thus less a matter of wilful, individual construction acts than psychological constructs that are collectively shared, entrenched and passed on to other members of the collective. There is a certain chance for reconstruction but the in-built barriers to fundamental change are, as we shall see, often difficult to surmount.

'Risk', 'threat' and indeed 'danger' can be conceptualised as social constructions that people mobilise to support and defend political, social and moral positions, as well as to define and maintain conceptual boundaries between Self and Other (Mackey 1999:111). Hence, 'danger', 'threat' and 'risk' are discursive devices used to construct certain political, social and moral positions as natural, 'common sense', and rational, whereas opposing positions are labelled as irrational, hazardous and disloyal. The positions constructed as normal and common sense are most often taken for granted and are thus rendered invisible. Only those phenomena that are deemed to be abnormal and contrary to common sense stand out—only they are seen.

In other words, notions of risk and threat co-construct an imagined 'normal' state of affairs that should be defended from perceived ills—whether it be a 'normal' or 'healthy' body at risk from disease or a 'healthy' and 'prosperous' nation endangered by outsiders or purportedly devious insiders. Perceptions of risk guide processes of inclusion and exclusion, and are highly normative in their consequences. They construct an ideal of 'normality' by defining abnormalities and dangers which are to be prevented, marginalised and averted. Take, for example, perceptions about national communities that are considered to be at risk; there, notions of risk draw on and reinforce axiomatic assumptions about the values that are central to the nation. By extension, risk perceptions perform the same function with regard to other communities of collective identification, such as those of religion, region, village or ethnic group (Mackey 1999:111-112).

Narratives About Risk

At a fundamental level, studying stories about immigrants and refugees in contemporary Western societies means studying discursive structures about socio-cultural risk that are prevalent among the general public. Human beings use stories of different kinds to make sense of their lives and of the world in which they live. Some stories reflect the basic values of day-to-day existence, and so they serve to unite people in assessing what is right and what is wrong, what is good and what is bad, and what differentiates their societies from those of others. Common stories are necessary to provide parts of the cement which holds people together. They provide assistance in interpreting what is going on and why, what collective decisions and judgments should be made, and what actions individuals within these collectives should take (Tilly 2002:27). Taken together, these stories comprise the collected ethos of different groups (Bar-Tal 2000), and they serve key functions in the everyday construction of collective identities.

Stories may alternatively be labelled 'narratives' and that is also the most common term used in scholarly literature. Margaret Somers (1994) discerns four dimensions in her useful conceptualisation of narratives, namely; ontological, public, meta and conceptual narratives. Ontological narratives are those that social actors use to make sense of their lives. They are used to define who we are which, in turn, is a precondition for knowing what to do. Ontological narratives, which are above all social and interpersonal, thus make identity and the Self fluid and developing rather than static and still. Public narratives, on the other hand, are attached to cultural and institutional formations larger than the single individual, and they range from the narrative of one's family to those of the workplace, church, government and nation. And on an even larger scale again, meta narratives refer to the master narratives in which we are embedded as contemporary actors. These can be about the 'epic dramas of our time': capitalism vs. communism; the individual vs. society, barbarism vs. civility and modernity vs. tradition. And finally, conceptual narratives are as a rule embedded in meta narratives and are those concepts and explanations that social scientists construct in their attempts to analyse social and political life. They affect the choices researchers make in defining key problems and analysing their results. For a while using this terminology, then, this study is chiefly about the public narratives encountered in the newspapers of local communities. They are stories about the national and the local and about those not deemed to be party to those collectives.

Importantly, Somers (1994:616) underlines that events conveyed by narratives cannot be analysed in an isolated fashion, but only as parts of a 'constructed configuration or a social network of relationships ... composed of symbolic, institutional and material practices.' Meaning cannot be attributed by categorisation alone (Whitebrook 2001:11). This has crucial implications for my study. My main source material is collected from newspapers, and stories retold by news media cannot and should not be seen in isolation, but must instead be regarded as component parts of larger stories. In other words, public narratives extracted for example from broadsheets should be seen as parts of the larger meta-narratives of societal discourse. The local material forms part of a national corpus of talking and writing (Grillo 2005:45) which in turn constitutes elements of even larger, transnational structures. Articles under scrutiny will therefore tell and retell sub-stories that shape parts of larger stories such as, for instance, those regarding the perceived superiority of the majority populations and the likewise perceived shortcomings of out-groups and their representatives.

The study of narratives was originally developed within and adapted for literary studies and the study of fiction, but the spectrum has successively been broadened. Even so, news media have surprisingly rarely been explicitly included among the genres considered suitable for the approach. Berger (1997:25), who has made valuable contributions towards widening the spectrum of narrative analysis, mentions for instance plays, comic strips and television programmes as promising contenders for such analyses. However, a common denominator for the paradigmatic studies of narrative as proposed by the followers of Lévi-Strauss (in Berger 1997:30) is that the focus should be on the meanings of the texts (as interpreted by the researcher) rather than on particular sequencings in the text, which was suggested by early textbooks on the theme. This would certainly qualify articles printed in newspapers for a narrative study. Indeed, Bal (1985:13) explicitly mentions news reports among the genres fitting for narrative analysis. And since this is precisely the kind of source material that I am focusing on, I am happy to tow this line. As pointed out by two authors in this field, 'we tend to understand the news as stories, and usually these are stories about people' (Gandy & Li 2005:72).

As we shall see, stories come in many different varieties: as stereotyped characterisations, as rumours and urban legends, and as more or less thinly veiled prejudicial structures in everyday discourse. The methodological approach taken in this study is thus to try to unravel these stories through the study of a local newspaper, which is taken to serve a key function for local people to define and develop the tenets of the collectives that they belong to. I shall return to this matter shortly.

Encountering Strangers—Obstacles to Integration

Despite the fact that transborder migration is a phenomenon that is at least as old as the modern state system, it has come to be regarded as one of the most potent and visible manifestations of the globalising influences of contemporary times. In periods of uncertainty and upheaval, this is wont to create negative reactions among majority populations. The matter is exacerbated by the fact that immigration on a larger scale tends to occur simultaneously with economic restructuring and social change (Castles & Miller 2003:15). Blaming the victim is a widespread psychological phenomenon and one variant of it is often at work in this context. Some of the symptoms of global mobility—immigrants—are often mistaken for the causes of the upheaval (cf. van Dijk 1993; Norman 2004). Such reactions constitute one of the most crucial aspects of study for analysts who wish to understand and assess obstacles for the integration of immigrants into everyday life in their new societies. I would argue that such a focus is absolutely crucial. Where there is no integration into everyday life one cannot speak about integration at all.

Integration itself is not an easy concept to use, however. In a collection of essays, Thomas Hylland Eriksen (2004) finds the concept of integration to be akin to words such as command and control, standardisation and planning and he argues that it gives connotations to 'joyless security'. In the world of integration, he continues, everything proceeds according to plan; the table tops are always made of laminate and the coffee cups are always made of plastic. I agree that, not least in the Swedish public debate, the word integration has started to become somewhat tainted. This is above all since it has come to denote one-sided adaptation in conformity with the majority's norms. Still, we are so far vainly looking for a better word. When I refer to 'integration', I simply have in mind a state of affairs where the immigrant functions in his/her new surroundings in such a manner that both the society of the majority and the immigrant are satisfied with the situation. In order for this condition to be met, the immigrant needs to be part of, and accepted in, the everyday. This is an absolute necessity. There may well be tinges of 'joyless security' to this, but since migration is most often somehow enforced, it is hard to imagine a situation when the immigrant would feel absolutely happy about the situation. It takes time to resettle, regardless of whether this takes place inside or outside one's country of birth and long-standing residence.

Moreover, a point that Eriksen clearly misses in his lucid criticism is that the concept still stands out in a favourable light when compared to the word denoting the strategy which was its policy predecessor in many Western states, namely 'assimilation'. According to these governmental strategies, migrants are expected to sink or swim in their new host countries, where sinking is the failure to adapt and conform to the prevailing mores, norms and ways of life of the majoritarian society. In such a case, the migrant will undoubtedly be attributed the role of an outcast. Conversely, if s/he is successful in assimilating, s/he will in many ways stop being her-/himself, as the immersion into majority ways of life nears completion. To succeed, one has to become invisible. In other words, succeeding is also tantamount to sinking. Or rather, the cost of remaining afloat in the majoritarian society is that the Self, as outwardly projected, is redefined in a most fundamental way.

Studying Risk in the Context of Globalisation

Globalisation has, for several years now, been a prominent catchword in the social sciences. And although different estimations have been made concerning the newness of the phenomenon, as well as a cornucopia of rival definitions of the concept, there is at least some agreement that globalisation is a process that deeply affects many, if not most, people's everyday lives, at least in the Western world. In Harvey's (1989) apt characterisation, globalisation is above all about a compression of time and space. We are subjected to more and more influences from all across the globe and we dispose of less and less time to take in and digest these changes. And so, if we can accept the basic premise that globalisation is affecting more or less everyone in the Western, if not the whole world, it then becomes clear that tremendous challenges are being posed to vast numbers of individuals and groups of people.

While city-dwellers have, to a great extent, been open to foreign influences for a considerable period of time, a number of studies have pointed out that majority- minority problems still abound in urban milieus (Gilroy 1987, Solomos 1988, Back 1996, Haavisto 2002), and indeed there are few signs to suggest that the situation is improving. However, things may stand differently in rural areas and small-town environments and, to date, there has been a deficit of studies devoted to problems in the countryside (cf. Ray & Reed 2005). This is what I hope to rectify through this study, which is geared towards these kinds of communities. Of course one cannot and should not assume a priori that things are worse and that existing clashes are more uncompromising in rural settings. The point is merely that, in order to be able to account for the potential similarities or differences between rural and urban milieus, the former first need to be accounted for.

Without wishing to repeat too much of the main tenets of the widely known discussion within the scholarly literature on globalisation, suffice to state here that global influences and the reassertion of local identities and belongings constitute two sides of the same coin. This is what lies behind Robertson's (1992) celebrated concept 'glocalisation'. On the one hand, the increased scope and pace of rapid communication networks, global travel, financial transactions and the like serve to erode traditional bases of belonging, most notably on the national level. In Castell's (1989) oft-cited phrase, the world of places is being replaced by the world of flows. The importance of physical territory seems to be decreasing and place is becoming less and less relevant for the definition of the space of human action and belonging. Consequently, the significance of national borders seems to be on the wane, with all the implications that this might have for the Westphalian international state system, which has for so long tacitly come to be understood as a given in the Western world (Waever & Kelstrup 1993).

On the other hand, this perceived squeeze on nation states, along with seemingly formidable and intrusive global influences, increase the individual's need for a secure foothold in his/her daily life (Kinnvall 2004). In a rapidly moving and transforming world, where many professionals are highly mobile or even rootless, there is an understandable urge to nurture and emphasise local identities, like the one of the block, the village, the small-town community, the region of residence or, often most notably, the nation. Here, national and local identity structures can be assumed to interact with and reinforce each other, thus combating the unknown, which one way or the other is perceived as emanating from the global.

To be sure, from a positivist's point of view—which I must confess not to share—globalisation literature has one inherent weakness; namely that the causes of globalisation, as well as the effects of the increasing assertiveness of the local and its sharpened adversity to strangers, are merely postulated and never proven in the traditional sense of the word. Indeed, this is a problem that goes with the territory in this genre of writing. And although this book will share this weakness, and may well be objected to on these grounds by some critics, it is an objection that I am happy to address. For all that we can aspire to do as social scientists is to come up with what are hopefully convincing lines of argumentation, and provide interpretations and perspectives to put forth in our capacities as researchers. This text constitutes my humble contribution to this end. The case of globalisation, with its effects on belonging and the reception of strangers, has been convincingly argued by several writers, and I for my part accept it as a postulate and a background context to my work.

To return to the vantage point of this chapter, however, the current stage of developments in the Western world is, according to Beck (1992), characterised by the abundant prevalence of risks, many of them long-term and man-made. Likewise, in Giddens' (1999:20-35) vocabulary, our times are fraught with risks of a hitherto never experienced magnitude and variety.   The globalising world,'has left some people feeling torn and lost' (Scholte 2000:226). It is a tall order for social scientists to try to delve into the possible consequences of feelings of this kind, but it is nonetheless necessary. For even if any attempt to locate arguments about socio-cultural risk requires addressing the vague and indeterminate, there is always a possibility that such risk discourses may spill over into more portentous arguments about threat and danger.

Globalisation, the Local and Multiculturalism

Compared to the original ideas that I had when I set out to undertake this research project, there is one important sense in which my expectations were not met. I had indeed expected more numerous and more vivid manifestations of nationalism to be found at the local levels that I studied. However, unambiguous articulations of national belonging turned out to be rare. What did take place, though, and did so rather often, were manifestations of local belonging where it often was rather unclear and unarticulated exactly what the 'local' comprised and on what levels of society its building blocks were to be found.

Moreover, discussing what is to be subsumed under the heading 'local', and whether or not it should be thought of as comprising belongings conventionally found at a local as well as a mezzo, or national level, one thing should be kept in mind. I would argue that in some sense the distinction might be deemed to be irrelevant 'out there', 'on the ground'. To begin with, the perceived defenders of cherished values and habitual modes of thinking may actually be less than aware of what levels these traditional structures should be located on. Furthermore, whether or not behaviour perceived as deviant is labelled as 'un-Swedish' or 'un-hometownish' is also of inferior significance. What really matters is that such behaviour is not judged to fit into the community of values defined by the in-group (cf. Tajfel 1982), and therefore may evoke defensive mechanisms. This is a variant of the familiar fact that it is hard to define what unites the in-group in positive terms, whereas it is far easier to determine what characterises the individuals and groups not deemed worthy of partaking in the community (cf. Petersson 2001). Suffice to say at this point that, at local as well as at national levels, entrenched values collude to produce reactions aimed at protecting the in-groups from perceived onslaughts from abroad. One could say that there is a local-national nexus at work, combating the global and the unknown, even if it is seldom articulated in this way in everyday discourse. Thus, although we may not encounter dynamics of nationalism head on in the field, we do come across the application of stereotypically negative images of strangers and, indeed, instances of at least unarticulated and latent racism.

When discussing those aspects of perceived present-day globalisation that seem to evoke fear and insecurity among people in their everyday lives, at least as exploited by more or less populist politicians (cf. Mackey 1999), the concept of multiculturalism comes to mind. For people living in rural milieus in the Western world, it may in some cases not have been until some 10-20 years ago that they started to perceive multicultural influences in their hometown settings. No longer can, for example, a country like Sweden be claimed to be an ethnically homogeneous state, if indeed that label was ever justified in the first place (cf. Norman 2004:206). This is a healthy and natural development, not least considering that it is a globalising world, but it might be hard to accept for some. Especially if one's individual career and day-to-day existence have given rise to disappointment and frustration, it may be temptingly easy to target marginalised immigrant out-groups as the sole source of misery.

Globalisation is a very vague concept for most people; it can be found and encountered everywhere, it is a phenomenon that is truly omnipresent, but this also constitutes part of the problem. The proverbial dog might well bark, but it is never really seen; its characteristics are nebulous. Multiculturalism is more tangible, it can be experienced in everyday life as representatives of the majority population meet people with different complexions, different colours of hair and different religious beliefs and, most typically perhaps, in the event of buying and tasting food originating from countries and cultures other than their own. It is easy, in other words, to connect the term to those immigrants that the majority population believes that it sees and discerns in the neighbourhood.

In this book, I shall use the term 'multicultural' in the same manner as Bhikhu Parekh (2000:6), who helpfully differentiates between the terms 'multicultural' and 'multiculturalist'. The former refers to any society that includes two or more cultural communities, whereas the latter connotes a prescription for a certain, liberally inspired policy aimed at promoting cultural groups other than the majority one—most often, however, on the terms of this majority. I shall use the term 'multicultural' in the neutral way that Parekh proposes. In other words, it will here express a mere statement of fact, that being that a society includes two or more cultural communities. With such a usage, I refrain from taking a stance in the debate on multiculturalism as an integrationist strategy.[2] Indeed, I prefer to concentrate on other battles, such as exposing dynamics of xenophobia, racism and distrust in tranquil settings, where they may not a priori be expected to occur.

Again following Parekh (2000:7), there is one factor that makes the multiculturalism of today more prevalent than that of yesteryear, even though it is not, as already mentioned, a novel phenomenon. In earlier periods minority communities far too often used to accept their situation and subordinate themselves to assimilation by dominant groups; fortunately such resigned practices are no longer as dominant as they once were. Thanks to the increasingly transnational spread of ideas and experiences, awareness has become heightened among these groups and they no longer resign themselves that easily to an inferior status. And since multiculturalism is so intimately and intrinsically bound up with different facets of globalisation, the result is that no society 'can remain self-contained and isolated' (Parekh 2000:8). People travel all over the world and material and immaterial goods and services cross borders with a hitherto unsurpassed speed and magnitude. Inevitably, and importantly, there will therefore also be those who feel forlorn and left behind, unable to match this pace.

Studying the Majority in Local Settings

As made obvious by the term 'minority studies', migrated or other minority groups have in academic history all too often been singled out for scrutiny, suggesting that they are deviant, exotic, or else warrant special attention. Indeed, according to this view, the deviant and the exotic have always seemed to be located elsewhere, or at any rate not among Us, the members of the majority. As observed by van Dijk (1987:15) and supported by others (Sibley 1995, Brekhus 2000), by neglecting to study majority-population views and attitudes, 'most White scholars in the humanities and social sciences have conveniently ignored this social problem, if not in their everyday life, then mostly in their academic work.' This is a shortcoming that the present study seeks to steer clear from. Indeed, my focus will be on the majority population. Such an approach makes it possible to assess and discuss the chief obstacles to integration and to the successful embracing of notions of diversity and multiculturalism (cf. Starnawski 2003:67). For I maintain that the greatest hurdles are to be found among members and structures of the majority, who are reluctant to let the 'outsiders' in.

There is already an established tradition to study how local communities cope with, or rather, respond to, challenges from the outside. Over the years, this line of research has most notably been pursued by sociologists and anthropologists. A classical study on a local community and its responses to the influence of perceived strangers is Norbert Elias' and John Scotson's (1999, new ed.) work on the reception of relative newcomers to the English suburb of Winston Parva in the 1960s. There were three residential areas in the suburb, the first one traditional and inhabited by the most well-to-do, while the other two were chiefly populated by manual labourers. The latter two were both established in the 1920s-1930s, but there was one big difference between them. The second residential area was mainly inhabited by people from Winston Parva itself, whereas the third one had above all attracted people from 'the outside', from London and from other cities. It had thus come to be labelled as an area for newly arrived and not yet established inhabitants of the community.

The Winston Parva study showed that it did not take much to become stigmatised in the local community and to be excluded from it. There did not have to be any ethnic markers, nor did there necessarily have to be any diverging class belongings. Not being a traditional town-dweller was enough to be branded an 'outsider', especially if one had moved in from London in search of employment and consequently ended up in the least prestigious residential area of Winston Parva. Community sentiments could be merciless and even exclude some of those individuals who already lived in the assumedly accepted areas. Those individuals who took to behaving aberrantly to prevailing norms could face tough times. In one such example, this 'strange' behaviour was represented by a woman who had recently moved into one of the established residential areas. On one particularly cold morning she decided to invite the garbage collectors in for a cup of tea. As it turned out, this was a fateful mistake, and the traditionally-minded neighbours hastened to brand her as a person of improper behaviour.

Elias and Scotson's study was a forceful reminder that the diacritica underlying choices of exclusion need not be based on ethnicity, religion, race or even class, even though there was certainly a class element to the exclusion mechanisms of Winston Parva. In our times, however, ethnicity is an oft-reiterated ground for exclusion. This is a finding confirmed by David May (2001) in his Elias/Scotson-inspired study on the stigmatisation of the economically weak and immigrant-dominated Nordstadt in Dortmund, Germany. He found that exclusion based on class-related, but also and mainly on ethnic, diacritica appeared to be a phenomenon that had expanded since several generations, but which had become particularly acute during the contemporary period. A recurring view among the majority population was that the inhabitants of Nordstadt were largely characterised by criminality and by a certain 'primitivity of mind'.

Even though the encounters between migrated groups and majority populations have tended to be quite uncompromising in small-town settings, much previous research has concentrated on urban areas (Gilroy 1987, Solomos 1988, Back 1996, Haavisto 2002, Dahlstedt 2005). However, the idea to concentrate on a rural, small-town community is for example pursued in a project by Katherine Fennelly (2005). In her study she has focused on Faribault—a rural town just south of Minneapolis—which has a growing proportion of Asian, Latino and African residents. In the context of the project, she has analysed patterns and instances of racism and discrimination, as well as conflicts arising from the immigration of culturally different newcomers to rural communities. Similarly, Tony Kushner (2003) studied local reactions among the residents of a British small-town by the name of Lee-on the-Solent with roughly 6 000 residents. There was a public outcry in the town against the idea of housing some 400 single male asylum-seekers on the premises of a former naval base in its vicinity. According to the prevailing sentiments, the asylum-seekers could be expected to bring crime, terrorism, drugs and sexual menace in their wake. Also, there was widespread alarm that house prices would be lowered as a consequence of their moving in. The campaign was initiated on the grass root level, but morally and financially it was supported by local political actors, and none of the political parties distanced themselves from the clamour. In a similar study, Ralph Grillo (2005) studied violent reactions in the small British community of Saltdean, which resulted in the responsible authorities changing their minds about localising a reception camp for asylum-seekers, a so-called induction centre, in the area.

Of course, ethnic and class-based markers can reinforce each other, but they need not do so at all times. In one case, for example, the ethnic diacritica seemed to be the strongest and the ones most difficult to overcome. In her study of the majority population's attitudes towards Asian immigrants in a contemporary British small-town nicknamed Greenville, situated near to the multiethnic city of Leicester, Katharine Tyler showed that ingrained prejudiced views about Asian immigrants were not easily rocked by the fact that certain individual migrants had reached high rungs of material affluence and acquired real estate in the most attractive residential areas. Rather, this seemed to provoke sentiments of envy and perceptions of unfairness among the settled majority. In everyday discourse among the suburb-dwellers, the Asians were being branded as cultural deviants and were excluded from the majority society. The majority population liked to think of their suburb as a village, epitomising the traditional, English and 'white' ways of life. Apparently, immigrants from Asia, and indeed, especially rich and successful immigrants, seemed to pose a challenge to their traditional mores, which is why they evoked such negative reactions. Middle-class membership could not be bought and paid for by sheer material affluence. Rather, it was acquired through tacit and evasive cultural knowledge, which was presumably the preserve of those belonging to the majority population. All else seemed to constitute the exceptions that proved the rule (Tyler 2003).

As this overview suggests, we may well be living in an age of hitherto unsurpassed magnitude of interrelations across national boundaries. Globalisation may well entail increasing openness for individuals reaping its harvests and enjoying its benefits first hand (Bauman 1998), but the local part of the glocalisation complex would seem to be more rigid. The 'nimby principle' (Hedetoft 2003:208)—not in my back yard—is often found to apply. In other words, resistance is likely to be encountered locally against globalising influences. As I have tried to argue, this is to a large extent due to vivid images of socio-cultural risk affecting cherished values of community life. But how do we proceed to analyse these kinds of local reactions? This is a subject to which I will turn in the next chapter.

Notes

1. On this score, Mary Douglas (1992:24) introduces different levels of risk: risk means danger, high risk means a lot of danger. In other words, high risk in her usage corresponds to 'danger' in mine. Thus our choices of wording differ here.

2. In a scathing criticism, for example, Hylland Eriksen (2004:157) writes that multiculturalism is only a millimetre away from apartheid in its practical consequences.

3. Stories, Strangers, Stereotypes, Scapegoats

Images shared with others constitute important components of the stories that are told and retold about perceived strangers. These images are socially constructed, and hence they stand to be deconstructed, reconstructed or reconfirmed in daily life, whenever fixity or change is called for. In defining images as cognitive and affective conceptual lenses, organising devices and information filters, I have elsewhere taken some issue with a prevalent tendency in the literature about images to define away affective factors from this theoretical domain (Petersson 2001:7). There is, however, another important trait on which I agree with the main tenets of the argument pursued within the cognitively oriented theoretical literature. Theorists within belief-system theory have often pointed towards the great degree of permanence that characterises images (cf. Petersson 1998:42). These are understood as self-reinforcing devices that structure incoming information to make it fit with prevailing beliefs. Information threatening to challenge existing beliefs is either discarded altogether or bent to fit with the existing body of knowledge. Images are thus considered 'change-resistant' (Elgström 2000:69) and are regarded as being 'perpetuated' (Hirshberg 1993:78) on a continual basis.

As a matter of course, images become more solidly entrenched regarding people with whom we frequently interact. We can base our findings about them on first-hand information, even though we naturally interpret it according to our own beliefs. Most of the time, we have a reasonably firm empirical basis for our conceptions of others around us. However, regarding those about whom we do not have first-hand knowledge, we are left to base our ideas on hearsay; that is, if we have reason to have such ideas at all.

Stereotypes as Frozen Images

We all know of examples in human history of collectives of peoples who are looked upon with suspicion from the outset, and who are not given the slightest chance to refute negative preconceptions about them. Obviously, prime examples are the plights of Jews and Roma people through centuries of maltreatment. In these cases, the images adhered to by different in-groups have turned into stereotypes which quite simply do not allow for change. And this is exactly what I would like to posit here, namely that a 'stereotype' can best be understood as a 'frozen image'. And it is these images that convey much simplified beliefs about individual characteristics on the basis of ascribed group belonging alone.

Stereotypes constitute, writes Bhabha (1994:82), a substitute and a shadow. This may have harmful consequences. As we all know from childhood, shadows of looming trees at nightfall are far scarier than the objects casting them. Also, a shadow frozen onto a wall will create a lasting impression, and may in this way mould assessments of the passers-by.[1] To be sure, an image that has been frozen in such a manner might of course, like the clock that has stopped altogether, seem to be correct at certain points in time (cf. Elias & Scotson 1999). The clock is obviously 'right' twice every 24 hours, but in the meantime it is either slightly or very much wrong, with potential detriments to follow.

Just as it is reasonable to hold that there is a spectrum of Others relevant to identity construction, ranging from good and benevolent to evil and malevolent (Harle 2000), there is reason to argue that stereotypes come in many different varieties, and that they need not necessarily be negative per se. Stereotypes with an at face value positive content can also be encountered (Törnquist-Plewa 2000:2). Riggins (1997:9) argues that stereotypes express both derision and desire. The well-known tendency of certain stereotypes to stress the exotic traits of Others might for instance indicate the latter characteristic. The objects of the stereotype are said to represent traits that members of the in-group majority either covet or deplore the loss of. Even so, being characterised as original, authentic, unharmed by civilisation or whatever traits may be bestowed upon the objects, is still very much about being denigrated and ascribed characteristics that are not to be found among the in-group of the norm-setters (cf. Sibley 1995).

Thus, the traits ascribed to the stereotyped Others are either coined as problems or as as something that is coveted, as either negative or positive, but, and this is the very crux of the matter, they are never depicted as neutral (Kristeva 1991:39). In order to bring this out, let me quote an example found in the local Swedish newspaper from which I have extracted the bulk of my empirical material. It contained a piece announcing a public lecture about Estonia, Latvia and Lithuania to be held in a small-town municipality: 'The Baltic states are not all in communist grey, they all host marvellous cultural treasures, wonderful architecture and virginal natural environment', the paper stated (*Smålänningen* 13 February 2002, p. 19). In other words, these neighbouring countries either amount to problems or amazing treasure troves, but they are never neutral, never quite like us.

What is it, then, that makes certain stereotypes stick? As mentioned above, most stereotypes are acquired not through first-hand acquaintance, but are instead picked up through mechanisms of hearsay, either conveyed through parents or other close relatives, the education system, or the media (Gilens 1999; Cohen 1987:18). By this token, individuals can subscribe to stereotypes about a certain group of people, even if they have never even met a single representative of that particular group (Gilens 1999:161; Hinton 1999; Törnquist-Plewa 2000:4).

Many analysts would argue that mass media seldom shape stereotypes *de novo*, but that they catch on to and reinforce ideas that are already somehow part of popular wisdom (Hartmann *et al* 1974; Wilson and Gutiérrez 1995; cf. Johansson 1998, Cohen 1987). Through the consistency of the stereotypes that they peddle, however, the mass media do have a significant impact when it comes to entrenching certain stereotypes in public awareness. We shall return to this subject shortly.

Stereotypes, then, are frozen images, which can in turn be positive as well as negative. Enemy images, which are prominently addressed in the cognitively oriented literature on images (cf. Harle 2000), precisely constitute one type of negative stereotype. An enemy image, however, goes further in its claims than the routinely encountered stereotypes of the stranger, who is depicted as different and deviant in some respects, but who is not necessarily seen to represent any major threat to the norms and mores of the community. Nonetheless, the enemy image feeds off and develops from the stuff that these more common stereotypes are made of (Hier 2003: 17). Or, to put it differently, whereas generally negative stereotypes connote risk, enemy images purport acute threat and danger.

There is evidently a spectrum working itself out here. There are linkages between the marginalised stranger and the fully-fledged enemy that feature in the public imagery of a community. Indeed, Wilson and Gutiérrez (1995:152) argue that, when analysing media reports on collectives and groups deemed not to belong to the majority population, one can discern different stages in the treatment of them. Most crucially, initial relative neglect is likely to lead successively into the ascription of threatening traits to the Others, which is then likely to lead on into some kind of confrontational phase. In other words, risk discourse is changed into the more ominous variants of communication about strangers: those denoting threat and imminent danger.

Enemies, Strangers and Scapegoats

The perceived presence of the enemy is antithetical to a fully embraced notion of security in the society of the majority (Hier 2003: 18). It would be counter-intuitive to be able to feel secure with ill-wishing enemies around. An enemy image represents a portentous and potentially hazardous mental construct, as it might prompt representatives of the in-group to take pre-emptory action and nip the growing threat, perceived as emanating from the Other, in its bud. However, an enemy image may also connote that the enemy is a formidable one, with which one would do wisely not to pick a fight. The image sustained in the latter case is not prone to lead into confrontation. But if the Other is perceived as weak, s/he might be in a precarious position. I would argue that this is frequently the case with individuals and groups of individuals who are subjected to scape-goating; more often than not, they have simply been chosen just because they are considered to be vulnerable.

Scapegoating constitutes a special kind of enemy image, and thus also of negative stereotyping. There is also here, then, a short distance between com-mon and reinforced stereotypes of this kind, on the one hand, and hostile action perceived as preventive, on the other. Several externalities influence the process. If feelings of frustration, uncertainty and wrath abound, the presence of scape-goating phenomena might produce a highly explosive mix. This is especially the case if the perceived enemy is indeed believed to be weak or at least as not yet having acquired all of his, her or their potential strength.

Stereotypes of strangers lie at the base of images indicating the presence of evil and hostile others. Given the right—or rather, very wrong—mix of contex-tual factors, the stranger may turn into an enemy in the public mind. The am-biguous figure of the stranger is always hard to come to terms with for the popu-lations of host societies since it is fraught with uncertainty in all its aspects. 'The ambient security focuses on the fear for personal safety; that in turn sharpens further, on the ambivalent, unpredictable figure of the stranger', writes Bauman (1998:142). From a psychological perspective the stranger is a dual challenger of identities, contesting as s/he does both the identity of the in-group as well as that of his/her own group of belonging, the latter of which is a challenge which is hard for many, if not most, people to face (Kristeva 1991:42). To be sure, am-biguous things and persons can seem very threatening (Douglas 2002:xi). They challenge fundamental norms and codes of conduct, and this is often very un-nerving.

Indeed, it may be tempting for hard-pressed individuals to try to explain un-certainty or at any rate, give it a face, by focusing on negative characteristics of strangers and give these prominence in their perceptions and assessments. 'A significant characteristic of someone classified as "them" is to let [him/her] be manifestly different from the surrounding society, to possess a feature that stands out and which can be stigmatised' (Argounova 2001:48-49). The stranger-turned-enemy is taken to epitomise all that is bad, inferior or deteriorat-ing in society. Again, if a society's perceived problems are seen as being con-nected to common roots—in this case, to the stranger-come-enemy—the pressure brought about by societal transformations may become easier to handle for groups of people under duress. Only rarely on a collective basis are such fights picked against towering windmills; instead it is much more convenient to turn on groups that are already marginalised and, at least comparatively speaking, excluded. As pointed out by Barber (1995:182): '"Foreigners Out!" is in Western societies an easier slogan to sell than "McDonald's Out!"'. Single, vulnerable groups are quite simply put easy prey.

Scapegoating is, according to Tatyana Argounova (2001:51) 'the process by which bad luck, diseases, misfortunes and sins are symbolically placed on an object, animal or person'. This definition is useful but has to be amended for the analysis of contemporaneous processes. Firstly, the victims of scapegoating most often need to be referred to in the plural. Secondly, and even more importantly, individuals performing the scapegoating are often quite convinced that the scapegoats are actually to blame for misfortunes of different kinds; there is in fact little that is symbolic about the process, at least in the way that it is perceived on the ground. Furthermore, even though animals, as will be discussed below, constituted the original target in ancient times, the attribution to creatures other than humans is a rare phenomenon in the contemporary Western world (although, as discussed in the Swedish debate on the issue, the fear of wolves in the northern part of the country constitutes an exception). Consequently, the amended definition that I propose would be that scapegoating denotes 'the process by which one or several persons are ascribed the blame for the incidence of bad luck, diseases, misfortunes and sins'.

The term 'scapegoat' derives from a practice described in the Old Testament, in which a high priest laid his hands on a goat that had been chosen by lot to take on the collective guilt of the assembled people, after which he let it loose in the wilderness (Mellema 2000, Kearney 2003). The people present at the ceremony were thus considered to be redeemed of their sins, which were all transferred to the animal. We can recognise the similarities between this and contemporary scapegoating processes: the scapegoat is 'invested with the internal malice of the community and then expelled into the wilderness, eradicating all perils of contagion' (Kearney 2003:28). Just as in the old days, people feel 'purified and solidified' once the process has been carried out (Cohen 1985:233). There is the familiar appeal of easy answers and easy solutions, and transferring blame from self to other is no doubt a rewarding enterprise for many actors involved.

One notable difference however emerges in a comparison between ancient and contemporary times. People witnessing the ancient ceremony could hardly regard the goat as an enemy per se; it was merely a vessel, an animal chosen at random to perform an important function. Religious convictions may well have singled out the creature as a bearer of evil and malice, but in that case this was due to spiritual or demonical infiltration from without. The animal in and of itself was not to blame. When we refer to scapegoating processes of today, where whole groups of individuals are targeted, it is hard to reach a conclusion other than that the scapegoats are being ascribed malevolent traits in and of themselves—i.e. they are not considered to be merely vessels but actual wrongdoers and culprits. And connected as they are to bad luck, disease, misfortune and sins, these collective scapegoats do take on the traits of an enemy. Scapegoat images go together with discourse of danger and are prone to prompt action alleged to be preventative. Needless to say, however, the actual term 'scapegoat' is not used by victimisers themselves, as this would imply the innocence of their victims.

Scapegoats, too, come in many different varieties and forms. They can be as diverse as the global financial community, the national administration in the state capital, small minority groups, or individuals associated with unfortunate events, such as those participating in sports activities which did not live up to the expectations of their audience. Swedish readers are likely here to think of the Swedish goalkeeper in the Olympic ice hockey tournament in 2002, whose relatives suffered a hard time at home because of the less than glamorous part he played in Sweden's unexpected defeat against Belorussia. The language employed by the critics was uncompromising and harsh, and terms such as 'national disgrace' were used in the discussion (cf. Petersson & Robertsson 2003:4). Football fans, on the other hand, may well remember the name of a certain Colombian defender, who was shot dead shortly after his return home after an unsuccessful game in the World Championship tournament of 1994, where he had happened to put the ball into the net of his own team. Such scapegoating phenomena are certainly intriguing to study in their own right, but in this book I will concern myself solely with the third example mentioned above, namely with those representatives of already vulnerable and marginalised minority groups who are perceived to represent negative phenomena, such as misery, criminality, contagious diseases and the like.

The groups selected by scapegoaters tend to be those that are the most simply available; they also tend to have some noticeable basic differences from the in-group and are quite probably also disliked from the outset (Douglas 1995:63, M. Douglas 1992:7, 87). Like conspiracy theories, enemy images can never be falsified. In view of information indicating the correctness of particular stereotypes, preconceived unfavourable impressions are corroborated. However, in cases of information not quite matching or even contradicting stereotypes, such news can conveniently be interpreted as merely affirming the cunning and conniving nature of the enemy/scapegoat. S/he is even devious enough to try to manipulate us into believing in her/his good intentions, or so the argument might run. As crisply stated by Mary Douglas (1992:9), 'if you want to cast blame, there are always loopholes for reading the evidence right'.

And so, once it has been cast in the image of an enemy, the presence of the targeted individual or group is just considered to be bad news to the majority population. 'The enemy's visitation on our borders is tantamount to impending pestilence', writes James Aho (1994:109). The scapegoated category comes to be regarded as impure, indeed as filth and excrements that should be flushed out by society as soon as possible (Sibley 1995, Aho 1994). The sooner the better; or otherwise the health of the majority is held to be in jeopardy. The stranger-turned-enemy tends to be associated with 'murder, epidemic and looting' (Bauman 1998:75-76). As long as these phenomena are relegated to a distant

'Third World', where they can be ascribed to the kind of people who Bauman (1998) labels 'faraway locals', this tends not to be regarded as a major problem by most people in the Western world. It is what happens once those faraway locals appear in our very midst that the real problems are likely to start and where notions of risk are translated into more tangible worries of imminent danger.

Stereotype Formation Dynamics

Negative stereotypes and enemy images are highly instrumental in upholding the borderlines that help collectives of people to establish and define their group identities (Sibley 1995, Bishop & Jaworski 2003, cf. Elias & Scotson 1999:71). It is, as already stated, easier for a group of people to agree on whom is *not* considered to be one of their peers than to establish the positive criteria for membership of the collective. This is why scapegoats, along with excluded groups in general, contribute to the reinforcement of feelings of togetherness among majority populations. This is also why, according to Girard, scapegoating constitutes 'the nominizing gesture par excellence, the very basis of both psychological and social order' (quoted in Aho 1994:116). Mary Douglas (2002:5) observes that 'it is only by exaggerating the difference between within and without, about and below, male and female, with and against, that a semblance of order is created'. The marginalised are essential for the very construction of the in-group Us.

According to Norbert Elias' (1999:xxxi) familiar observation, there is a certain logic to the way that established, well-situated groups form the views of themselves and of the socially excluded collectives deemed not to belong to them. In a *pars pro toto* manner, the established groups ascribe to themselves the characteristics of their brightest and most virtuous members, while they brand the marginalised groups with the traits found amongst their most troublesome and disorderly. In both cases, the parts taken to represent the whole tend to be equally small minorities. Stereotypes certainly do not describe reality; they distort it (Törnquist-Plewa 2000:3).

Perennial outsiders, such as the Roma people, have traditionally served to knit insiders closer together. Regardless of whether they have been depicted as exotic and close to nature, or whether they have been vilified outright, they have clearly served this function. 'The Gypsies are nearer to the animals than any race known to us in Europe', decried a British chronicler in the 19th century' (cited in Barany 2002:63). Throughout the centuries, the Roma people have been stigmatised as 'lazy, uninhibited, deceitful, dirty, unreliable, and prone to theft and other criminal behavior' (Barany 2002:63). And in the process, the in-groups have been left to feel more confident about their own cohesion and perceived excellence. As so succinctly put by Kearney (2003:33), 'for saints to remain saintly, strangers [have] to be scapegoated'.

The stories of the majority population become reinforced by their iterated retelling and recounting. These stories may of course concern the perceived excellence of the in-group itself, but more often than not they are tales of the perceived deviance of the out-groups. However, challenges may be seen to emanate from the counter-narratives of these marginalised groups. 'Counter-narratives of the nation that continually evoke and erase its totalizing boundaries (...) disturb those ideological manoeuvres through which "imagined communities" are given essentialist identities', observes Bhabha (1990:300). Consequently and in order to face this challenge, the narratives of the majority are invoked and recounted with greater and greater degrees of assertiveness and persistence, so as to combat any perceived risks emanating from the groups that are not part of the majority Us. There is thus a power struggle going on, but most of the time it is on unequal terms.

The likelihood of minority groups to be Othered and, indeed, the potential of scapegoats to make majority populations aware of what unites them increases in times of unrest and trouble, since fear of danger clearly tends to strengthen the lines of division in a community (Douglas 1992:34). In turbulent times, there is a strong tendency to reclaim one's perceived roots, to try to re-embrace group identities felt to be deeply entrenched. Human history is replete with such examples. In the Middle Ages, someone had to be blamed for the scourge of the Black Death; and so the Jews came in handy. Similarly, women were once unceremoniously thrown overboard in storms to placate the weather-gods. But one need not travel this far back in time to encounter phenomena of collective guilt-ascription. Among the news reports of events occurring in the immediate wake of the terrorist attacks in the United States on September 11, 2001, there was a disturbing item about a white, middle-aged American, who in a blinding fit of rage over what he had just watched and heard on the news, walked down to the Arabic kebab-owner on the corner, and shot him dead on the spot. We do need to understand these phenomena better; otherwise we will never be able to prevent them from happening.

Description and illustration are precursors of understanding. Before closing this chapter, I therefore turn to a vivid illustration of how a perceived defence of cherished values may bring scapegoating in its wake. The case concerns racially motivated riots—Russian media referred to them as pogroms—that took place in Moscow during the autumn of 2001.

The Tsarytsino Events[2]

On 30 October 2001, a lynch mob, consisting of some 300 young people, stormed a market situated next to the Moscow metro station of Tsarytsino. Outdoor vendors, the majority of whom were presumed to be originating from the Caucasus, were attacked by the mob. After a while, the police arrived at the scene and fired warning shots, but more than 100 attackers escaped and continued on to the Kakhovskaya metro station, where they targeted a nearby hotel. The attackers yelled racist slogans and assailed all dark-skinned persons that they could come across—Chechens, Armenians, Roma, Indians and Afghans. During the atrocities, at least 3 people were killed by the mob, and about 15 people were severely wounded. According to the first reports, the mob consisted primarily of football hooligans. Later, however, it appeared that there was a hard core consisting of members of a Russian neo-Nazi party.

Analysing the events, Ramazan Abdulatipov, a deputy of the Federation Council (the Upper House of the Russian Parliament) and a former cabinet minister for nationality issues, cautioned that the 30 October events were a sign of an impending national collapse. The actions of the lynch mob should be assessed as something taking place in the wake of September 11, he argued. Thus, the carnage was an expression of Islamophobic sentiment that was spreading through the country after the terrorist attacks against the Twin Towers and the Pentagon.

The leader of an ultra right-wing party came to the defence of the lynch mob. The actions were, he claimed, 'a natural reaction among young people to the massive influx of non-Russians to Moscow.' According to the decrepit logic of conspiracy theories, he discerned the hands of several sinister groups of enemies behind the immigration situation, which had made those young people react with violence. It was time, he said, for 'the consolidation of the Russian people ... to stop the expansion of Jewish pan-Americanism'. The notorious leader of the so-called Liberal Democrats, Vladimir Zhirinovskii, tried in a similar fashion to exploit the events for his purposes. The incident, he remarked, showed how necessary it was to 'cleanse Moscow' from 'criminal groups consisting of people from the south'. Not going to these extremes, but still hinting at the same problematique, Communist Party leader Gennadii Ziuganov said the terrible actions should serve as a wake-up call to Russia because the country did not have 'a normal nationality policy'. Thus, the blame was in several comments transferred from the actual perpetrators of the crimes to the very victims themselves.

In essence, according to these arguments, the violent extremists had merely taken basically commendable action in order to defend Moscow against the influx of foreign elements. A street-level participant of the actions, a skinhead, expressed himself precisely along such lines. The participants of the violent acts were just 'ordinary Russians fed up with foreigners', he said, going on to add that he did not care that people were killed during the recent pogrom. Appalling as the latter statement might be, it still did not match the result of an informal call-in poll conducted by TV6. There it turned out that 87 per cent of the Muscovite respondents actually supported the actions of the pogrom participants (Taibbi 2001). One Muscovite witness to the Tsarytsino events explained why: 'The Russians have to defend themselves against the unbridled ways of the blacks.[3] They just walk about here on our lands, hands in their pockets, fiddling with their money'. He was seconded by another man, who argued that 'it is necessary to apply a little pressure on the Caucasians,[4] otherwise they become too self-assured' (Ivashchenko 2001). Statements like these bespeak the popularity of anti-Caucasian sentiments in Moscow and Russia (Kisriev 2004), and might also go some way towards explaining the aforementioned statements by high-profiled, vote-maximising political figures like Zhirinovskii and Ziuganov.

The Context of the Riots

Enemy images and scapegoating phenomena do not arise suddenly and out of the blue. They are no doubt social constructions, but they are also inherited and even reinforced by successive generations. These constructs find their institutionalised expressions in legends and myths that are told and retold by parents, the media and in history books and they figure in habitual modes of thinking and reasoning. They have a cumulative effect and possess formidable longevity, due to perennial and repeated chains of reconstruction. Again, as enemy images and stereotypes of scapegoating can never really be falsified, all evidence collected from the archives of popular wisdom can be used as corroborating evidence.

The fault lines defining the conflict between Russians and Chechens date back about 150 years. Indeed, both sides in the current secessionist war have made consistent use of the old conflict patterns and mutual enemy images. I have elsewhere analysed how Vladimir Putin's landslide victory in the 2000 presidential elections in Russia was primarily due to his renewed war effort against the Chechen separatists (Petersson 2001). Prior to his election, several concerns had been voiced about the pending political collapse of the country. This became a prominent theme not least regarding the increasingly rambling and irrational statements made by his ailing predecessor, Boris Yeltsin. Major themes of concern were the increasingly separatist tendencies in different regions of the Federation; the mounting and seemingly ever-present political and economic crisis; the particular threat emanating from Chechnya and the northern Caucasus; Islamic fundamentalism; organised crime; and, finally, the perceived impotence of Yeltsin's political administration. And the ingenious thing about the Chechnya campaign was that, in one masterstroke, it took care of all these concerns. It combated the regionally specific threat, it countered separatism and Islamic fundamentalism, and it dealt indirectly with organised crime, as Chechnya had for several years been perceived as a hothouse for mafia activities. In its introductory phase, the forceful war effort—which was launched, it should be recalled, against the backdrop of devastating terrorist attacks on apartment buildings in Moscow and other Russian cities and towns during the summer and autumn of 1999—also stood in stark contrast to the unsuccessful first war on Chechnya during the period 1994-1996, and above all to the Yeltsin administration's subsequent wavering on the issue. Finally, since Putin was at times criticised for not having a proper political platform, or even a political programme indicating his preferred policies for dealing with the severe economic and social crisis in the country, the Chechnya campaign had the tactical advantage of buying him time to consider these matters at a later stage. In sum, Chechnya was perfect. And Chechens seemed to be the ideal scapegoats for welding the Russian people together. Not entirely convinced of what united them, Russian citizens could at least be pretty sure of whom were not eligible to take seats in their midst. By transferring the blame for all the present ills of the Russian Federation onto this scapegoated category of people, uncertainty could be reduced, and the continued weakness of the country-heir to the once-superpower, the Soviet Union, could be accounted for. And so, the situation was ideal for everybody but the Chechens.

It was argued above that enemy images and images of excluded Others tend to be associated with patently negative phenomena, like crime, disease, filth and excrement. Putin himself underlined such connotations through his well-known and brusque assertion in 2000 that his preferred policy towards the 'Chechen bandits' was to 'wipe them out in the shit-house' (Jack 2004:125). Thus, in a campaign against bearers of banditry, uncleanliness and filth, there were no ameliorating circumstances; no tears were to be shed. Rather, actions intended to 'mop up', 'clean up' or whatever metaphor that may have been used, were commendable and praiseworthy, as they promised to rid society of a polluting scourge.

The Russian example is admittedly an extreme one. But tendencies towards employing similar modes of thinking prevail in most places and countries of the world, indeed maybe everywhere. I will soon proceed on to other, less dramatic sites for the manifestation of such universal trends. First, however, it is time to focus on what may amount to the most important articulator thereof, namely, news media.

Notes

1. Indeed, more than 10 years after my visit to the Hiroshima museum devoted to the atomic bomb cataclysm, a frozen shadow on a wall is still my most vivid memory, as it left the most lingering impression.

2. See Petersson 2003 for a fully footnoted account.

3. The word 'blacks' is Russian street-level slang for people originating from the Caucasus.

4. NB that the term 'Caucasian' here reflects the Russian usage and denotes people originating from the Caucasus, and not 'white', which would otherwise be the standard English usage.

4. News Media, the Mundane and the Depiction of Strangers

The Russian examples above illustrate just how far things can go if stereotypes and enemy images are left to fester in an environment of political and economic uncertainty and even turmoil. Nonetheless, more tranquil and peaceful settings also have their share of problems, albeit to a considerably less dramatic extent. They are low-key and of low intensity. However, as explained above, such non-drastic everyday perceptions of the Self and the Other provide the very cognitive and emotive bases necessary for hot versions of self-assertion and other-denigration to erupt. Indeed, it is imperative to also study the stories that majorities tell about minorities in their everyday, non-dramatic settings, as well as the socio-cultural risks that these purportedly bring. This is, as should have become clear by now, also the main endeavour of this book.

In this study I therefore deal with what are, for the most part at least, rather mundane texts that tell us little out of the ordinary. The stark contrast to the Russian example recounted above is fully intentional. My ambition is to show that phenomena such as enemy images, negative stereotyping and latent scapegoating are also prevalent in peaceful and seemingly harmonious settings. Indeed, risk discourses are abundant there and, as already mentioned, they have the potential to develop into discourses of danger and threat.

The Importance of the Mundane

People make sense of their everyday existence and mark their boundaries of normality through the different stories that they tell about deviators in different respects. These stories are a way of handling uncertainty and risk perceptions; many of them share the same central building blocks and narrative structures. 'People's perceptions of risk are situated within the context of routinized and normalized local order and the production and functioning of everyday living', writes Hier (2003:13). The unknown is thus turned into something which is still strange, but at the same time strangely familiar in its strangeness. In this way, the perceived abnormal is pressed back and held at bay, and by granting the unknown facets that are recurring and somehow familiar, ambivalence is turned into familiarity, and familiarity is indeed a workable way to address the scary features of unknown risks and dangers. Nonetheless, these vague threats all too often attain familiar faces: namely those of the immigrants.

Voices abound when it comes to the necessity of studying story-telling in the everyday context. As Ekecrantz & Olsson remind us (1998:28), it is the 'unremarkable' texts which may tell us the most about our contemporary times, since they function as mirrors of the age and time in which they were written. Brekhus (2000) argues that 'in failing to take the ordinary as seriously as the extraordinary, social science has produced a distorted picture of the social world'. And Kristeva (1991:3) underlines that 'it is precisely the commonplace that constitutes a commonality for our daily habits'.

In a similar vein, Brekhus (2000) suggests that studies of the religious practices of only *modestly* religious people can provide insights that are more applicable to broad social studies than those that research on more pronouncedly religious groups is ever able to supply. Similarly, if related to the fields of nationalism and collective identity, it is in many respects the banal nationalisms (Billig 1995) and their manifestations that tell us most about the characteristics of nationalism in general.

The everyday, the mundane, is what 'remains after one has eliminated all specialized activities' (Harris 1999 as cited in Kallus 2004:345). Intuitively, this does not sound very interesting. Given a second thought, however, it most certainly is. Local manifestations of patterns of power and domination in the everyday world have thorough-going significance for the societies in which we live. Indeed, it is the fine threads of routine practices that make up the overall fabrics of the social order. And it is at the local level that we as analysts have to commence any study of how these webs of power are woven and how they play themselves out. As Hier (2003:5) puts it, 'the affirmation of social order is situated in the realm of locality, forged through the production of everyday living'. Routine and mundane practices matter and they provide useful focal points that can profitably be studied in order to get at the very core of social practices that form people's day-to-day existence (cf. Kallus 2004). In other words, if one wishes to analyse patterns of societal responses to pressures for change from the outside world, the everyday is a natural and important starting point (cf. Ellegård 2001).

Everyday Prejudice

The subject of everyday prejudice will be central to the following chapters. In dispelling the notion that prejudiced thinking is only the trait of a troubled minority of people, Billig et al (1988) showed that most people in everyday situations display a mix of prejudiced and unprejudiced thinking. Even 'ordinary people', who would find the notion of joining or even sympathising with ultranationalist, xenophobic political parties abhorrent, are prone to expressing a large amount of negatively stereotyped thinking and thus underwrite the perceived salience of boundaries between Us and Them (cf. Grillo 2005, Norman 2004). This is akin to van Dijk's (1987) line of thought that all white people in the privileged West are in essence racists. As argued by Billig et al (1988) and others, persons who express ideas that are markedly prejudiced and, indeed, even racist, can nonetheless stress their desire to conform with socially approved norms of non-racist discourse by simply adding familiar disclaimers such as 'I am not a racist, but...' and 'I am not prejudiced, but...'. Thus covered, they can then proceed to elaborate on thinking that definitely betrays a prejudiced slant. But, and this is the point advanced by Billig et al, the disclaimers need not be simply window-dressing; most frequently, they are actually sincerely meant. As a rule, therefore, prejudice and racism seem to be located outside the Self (Billig et al 1988: 109). No-one admits—probably not even to themselves—to being a racist, nor to being a bearer of prejudiced thinking.

This simultaneous co-existence of prejudice and aversion to it makes the phenomenon of prejudice much more difficult to counter. To put it differently, it is not the ideas and sentiments of the minority few representing the 'unambiguously prejudiced' which is the main societal problem. Rather, it is the views of the vast majority, those who Billig et al (1988) fittingly label as the 'reasonably prejudiced', that represent the real crux. It is precisely the views of these broad segments of the population that get entrenched in daily routines and practices and inhibit the integration of immigrants into the everyday life of our societies. It is thus for good reason that this study is focused on the views of those who are assumed to be 'reasonably prejudiced', the large and predominantly silent majority, as opposed to the vocal minority of overt xenophobes. The focus of this study is therefore mostly on 'the gentle folks', to borrow Kushner's (2003: 268) phrase. They are interesting exactly for that very reason, in that they constitute the mainstream; they are neither deviant nor radical nor ultra vocal. Furthermore, exclusionary practices performed by the gentle, decent folks are probably far worse to bear by those subjected to them than the variant performed by extremist xenophobes, whose words and deeds may instead serve well to knit the excluded groups closer together. To use an expression prevalent in the Swedish political debate a couple of decades ago, it may well be the 'tyranny of small steps' that in the end leads to the most depressing results for those affected. Indeed, most people probably find it easier to be singled out for abuse by hooligans than by gentle and decent folks.

News Media and Minorities

Mass media provide most crucial building blocks of the majority of people's visualisation of the world. Essentially, they construct, co-construct, develop and maintain certain shared visions of reality. In brief, the media matter (Fiske 1996), and this will be shown throughout the study.

In general, mass media function 'as a significant forum for the strategic deployment of dominant community values' (Moon & Nakayama 2005:104). More specifically, they constitute continual sources of information and points of view about minorities (van Dijk 1987, Pietikäinen 2003). Indeed, mass media constitute the arena where stereotyped beliefs in society about immigrants and refugees are most clearly expressed and notions of nationhood and the concomitant categorisations of in-groups and outliers are most visibly constructed (Lynn & Lea 2003; Starnawski 2003, Bishop & Jaworski 2003).

In low-contact areas, where people of the majority group do not tend to have frequent encounters with representatives from other ethnic groups and cultures, knowledge structures about minorities are often primarily based on information from mass media. Sometimes, as pointed out by Hartmann and Husband in their seminal study of the 1970s, the media can be the *only* source of information in such milieus (Hartmann & Husband 1974:92, cf. van Dijk 1987:163, Haavisto 2003). The kind of small-town communities studied in this book are less prone to display a multicultural mix of population than are metropolitan areas. And where personal experience is lacking, people can fill in some of the gaps by consuming information offered by news media outlets. Again, hearsay acquires a prominent role.

Of course one might question the degree to which there are any real low-contact areas left in the globalised Western world of today. For even if this is an observation made from the vantage point of a perennial city dweller, which can make it easy to forget about the persistent homogeneity of structures in rural areas, settlement patterns have certainly changed since the time that Hartmann and Husband performed their study. Today, many of or even the most rural settings in the modern Western world are at least to some extent multicultural. That aside, it is *not* the case, however, that mass media have become less important in the past 30 years when it comes to impacting on prevailing thoughts and perspectives about societal phenomena and processes, among them minority groups (cf. McQuail 2000). Indeed, contemporary media do reinforce prevalent distinctions between in-groups and out-groups and, thus, strengthen notions of what is to be considered normative and normal as far as membership in different collectives are concerned (Bishop & Jaworski 2003:267).

Why Local Media?

In this study, a predominant local newspaper has been selected as the chief inroad to studying majority-minority relations. It is a central argument here that the local news media represent, as well as provide, an outlet and a mouthpiece for elites belonging to the majority population. They are inspired and used by these groups and contribute towards their prevalence and importance in the local community.

Still, the focus on a *local* newspaper may seem odd to some readers. Are the local media not losing their significance in an age where televised news and Internet sources have acquired a central position for meeting the news preferences of the consumers? I would tend to answer both yes and no to this question. Yes, because audiences today tend to rely on these newer forms of media for information on global media events. An opinion poll performed in the United States some years ago, for example, indicated that 70 per cent of the respondents relied on television for their daily consumption of news (Gilens 1999:129). To be sure, most readers would certainly not turn to the local media to be updated on national events. Concerning local affairs, however, matters are different, as readers do rely on local media for local news (Nygren 2001:52).

Daily newspapers still constitute the most important popular source for information-gathering about the local community, and local newspapers are as a rule highly trusted by their audiences (Larsson 1998, Weibull 1995, 2000a). I remember from my own childhood in the 1960s that what was printed in the local newspaper in my small-town community was widely regarded as spelling out the indivisible Truth. Of course, things have changed since then, but I do believe that local news media retain a strong position, especially in the countryside. In small-town settings, like the ones we are researching here, the local media maintain a particularly strong position in the local community, precisely because they, in contradistinction to national newspapers, focus exclusively on local news. They do what they are good at and are duly rewarded, as local news are prioritised by the readership (Nord & Nygren 2002:35).

In this study, the local media will be regarded as having dual roles; they are both constrained by societal discourses at the same time as they influence them and contribute to defining their main tenets. They reflect the sentiments of the local environment at the same time as they construct and reconstruct them (Kratz 1995:55, Pietikäinen 2003). Media thus constitute an arena at the same time as they make up a crucial actor in its own right on this very arena (Petersson & Carlberg 1990). This dual perspective is adjacent to the perennial academic debate of whether mass media should be regarded as representing reality or constructing it (Ekecrantz & Olsson 1998). According to the first ideal, journalists merely transport and pass on the news items to the consumers. They do so conscientiously, being fully aware of what they are doing. They are thus almost independent of society at large; they are situated, as it were, above and beyond it, ready to be at the disposal of the audience, which is in turn in dire need of their elucidation. As the editors of *Smålänningen* told me during our conversation, 'we do not construct reality, we report it' (interview Gustafsson).

When addressing how the media construct reality, on the other hand, there is a quite familiar aspect to keep in mind, namely what can be called the media logic of operation. Since editors and journalists share an interest in selling as many copies of their newspaper as possible, they will try to make their stories more interesting and compelling than those of their competitors. There will therefore be an in-built slant in favour of the dramatic, the pointed, the personalised and, indeed, the simplified (Hernes 1978, Brune 2004). This aspect must of course be borne in mind when analysing any news reports dealing with the subjects of immigrants and risk.

However, the effects of this media logic on a local newspaper, such as the one that is under scrutiny in this study, should perhaps not be exaggerated. Firstly, it is the matter of a *local* newspaper, whose main task is precisely to report on the mundane and the non-dramatic. Secondly, local papers in Sweden tend to have few serious competitors, apart from the national broadsheets and tabloids. Swedish local papers usually enjoy a near monopoly status when it comes to reporting on local news, since the local markets tend not to be large enough to absorb more than one or two newspapers at a time. Thirdly, with the exception of the national tabloids, Swedish newspapers are typically not sold by the copy. People in Sweden generally subscribe to their daily newspaper six months or a year in advance. Thus, single scoops and reports about dramatic events are not prone to have an immediate effect on the sales of the paper.

The perspective advanced in this study, however, is less concerned with the representation or construction of certain news items as such; rather my preoccupation is with the ideas that lie at the basis of the news reports. These cognitive and attitudinal structures are widespread and culturally shared. They are multiplied and reflected through representations that, although certainly deliberate at times, remain more or less unbeknown to the writers of the articles and the editors most of the time.

I would argue that the media can be regarded as mirroring devices that reflect societal beliefs (cf. Bar-Tal 2000). The mass media are social institutions integral to the society in which they operate (cf. Hartmann et al. 1974:92), and the influence that the surrounding society brings to bear on them cannot be defined away. Nor can of course the influence of the newspaper on the local community be disregarded. Whatever prevalent modes of argument exist about issues such as immigration and multiculturalism in society at large, they will be represented and reflected in the local news media. The stories that are told and retold at work sites and kitchen tables will thus undoubtedly find their way to the news pages.

Moulding the Public Consciousness

Theorists dealing with the phenomena of nationalism may agree on precious little, but most of them would subscribe to the idea that the media play a very prominent role in influencing the popularly held national imaginary. Influential writers such as Benedict Anderson (1983) and Michael Billig (1995) have been elaborate in advancing ideas why the media are so important in the construction of communities, most notably national ones.

According to a widespread metaphor, a newspaper constitutes a 'public square', where political discussions are held and politics actually made (Nygren 2001, Weibull 2000b). Similarly, Hier and Greenberg (2002:494) see the media as a discursive space where political agendas are constituted and (re)figured. The media play an important role when it comes to setting, or at the very least, influencing these agendas. The daily newspaper is the 'central medium of orientation, the medium which inserts order into daily life' and the device which 'brings order to time and space' (Weibull 2000b).

Thus, the mass media in general are important players on the scene that they themselves constitute and co-construct. This is even more pronounced for the local media. Being active in the local community, local news media journalists tend to find themselves in a position where they are expected to commit themselves and proclaim a stance. They are wont to be more actively engaged than the national media journalist occasionally writing about an event taking place in a local community (Sandlund 2002:16). Therefore, local media representatives more frequently tend to assume the positions of agenda-setters and agenda-shapers in local affairs than their national counterparts do. However, the media actors need not at all times be aware that this is what they are doing. They may equally well believe that they are conscientiously reporting on 'reality as it is', just as the editors of *Smålänningen* did.

Indeed, the two principal perspectives of media as an actor and the media as an arena for action interact. Individual journalists may or may not therefore be aware that they are contributing to the entrenchment of certain beliefs, prevailing modes of expression and popular images (Erjavec 2003). What is in the making here is the kind of influence through subtle means that Billig (1995) has written so astutely about. Certain items and distinctions are taken for granted and accepted as true. One well-known and prominent example of this phenomenon is the subdivision of the world into home and abroad, and the congruent separation of the newspaper into pages dealing either with domestic or international news. As readers, we have become so accustomed to this order of things that, more often than not, we tend not to question it at all. And so, the daily newspaper contributes to the delimitation of the national as well as the local discursive space, geographically as well as mentally (Johansson 1998:97).

Counter-examples can no doubt readily be found, however. Being a resident of the border region between Sweden and Denmark, I have been able to see the many different ways in which the ideas of an intra-EU, transnational region with successively phased-out borders have increasingly manifested themselves in daily life, especially since the construction of the Öresund Bridge between the two countries (cf. Falkheimer 2004). Thus, my daily newspaper nowadays carries, as a regular feature, an amalgamated section on Skåne (the southernmost province of Sweden), Denmark and the Öresund region. So, the everyday world is depicted in quite different ways than it used to be, say, 10 years ago. However, this example again bespeaks and supports the argument about how the media impinge on the everyday construction of the world around us.

All of this is not to suggest that the media shape our impressions and views of the surrounding world from scratch. As argued earlier, they rather serve to reinforce and consolidate views that are already prevalent in society. Fundamental beliefs about the world and individuals and groups acting in it tend to be established during upbringing, education and, to a certain degree, in early professional life. The mass media take over from the early influences of school, religion, parents, siblings and companions (McQuail 2000: 64). Most people are likely to have beliefs that originate from channels other than the media, but the media serve an important role in convincing their readers that their preconceptions are justified and in some sense true. It has to be remembered that individual, fairly non-dramatic news items rarely change views that are firmly established and entrenched. Rather, it takes portentous, dramatic events to rattle them (Törnquist-Plewa 2000). As maintained by Guillaumin (1974:81), it is normally a matter of a 'slight oscillation around fixed points'. This is not to deny that 'the cumulative effect of many stories over a period of months or years may nonetheless be large' (Zaller 1992:311).

Picking up on the metaphor of media as a public square and bringing together the two above-mentioned principal perspectives—the media as a mirror of societal beliefs and as an arena for action, vs. the media as constituting actors—I will posit that the local newspaper can be regarded as a discursive marketplace in the local community. Multifarious merchandise is on display there, and the buyer/reader is on the face of it free to decide whether s/he wishes to buy the goods from the vendor or not. The more of a certain item there is on display, the more one can surmise that it is in demand, or that the prospective buyers at the very least will go home with pretty clear ideas of what they should buy in order to be regarded as part of the community Us. They may not actually have bought any goods from the market, but without their knowing it, they may have become more inclined towards certain future purchases during their stroll across the square. They may also have made their purchases seemingly out of their own free will, but they are nonetheless often prompted by forceful cognitive and emotive structures that they may not even be dimly aware about. Or, to use an analogy used by Thomas Hylland Eriksen (2004) in another context, if the milieu is instead likened to the one of a self-service cafeteria, a substantial part of the customers' orders will have been placed well before they actively start to fill their trays. The vendors, among them editorialists, news journalists and writers of letters-to-the-editor, have deliberately brought certain goods to the market, and they are certainly aware that they are selling them. They may be less aware, however, why they take it for granted that a certain kind of apple should always be represented in their stock or why their goods tend to be arranged in certain patterns and structures and not in others. They sell what they sell because of personal choices, but they are not always, if ever, aware of all the underlying aspects that have prompted them to make these choices.

Newspaper Sections and Journalistic Roles

It is common to differentiate between three kinds of journalistic roles, which can be regarded as signifying different discursive positions that are active in this overall writing and communication process. Olsson (2002:53-54) labels them as editorialists, news journalists and observers, and goes on to argue that the editorialists participate in 'the game of politics', the news reporters report about them, and the observer comments on them from a distance. I would maintain, however, that while these roles certainly represent different genres of journalism and different linguistic styles, it is not fruitful to separate any of these categories from 'the game of politics', since all of them surely take part in this game.

It is also debatable whether it is justified to uphold the traditional distinction that the editorials express the official line of the newspaper, whereas the news pages pass on reports about objectively mediated news. Flowerdew et al (2002) observed great divergences in messages conveyed by different sections of newspapers in Hong Kong. Whereas the editorials told one, liberal, story about migration policies and multiculturalism, the news pages and other sections all but overturned this message by arguing in quite different and decidedly less welcoming directions. As aptly put by Flowerdew and his associates (2002:343), it is a pertinent question to ask what department should be seen as representing the 'true institutional ideology' of the newspaper. Several studies about media consumption have shown that readers of local newspapers prioritise local news pages over editorials (Weibull 1995:78). Therefore, it may make little difference what the editorialists actually write unless their pieces are read by a broader audience. Thus, it is perhaps even fair to say that it is the news stories rather than the editorials that will be brought home to the readers as the main channels that pass on the most important messages of their local paper.

As will be further argued below, it is also of importance to study the letters-to-the-editor section, since views expressed there are quite likely to be noticed and read, and may have a lingering impact on readers' minds. The letters section comprises an interesting blend of private thoughts and public debate, of everyday discourse and mediated discourse (Lynn & Lea 2003:430). Ordinary readers are given the floor, albeit with certain restraints: the contents of the letters are still partly formed, or at least reined in, by the editorial policy of the newspaper. Letters that are too blatant will end up in the dustbin (Wahl-Jorgensen 2004).

The letters section has frequently been assessed as a central public forum essential for the workings of a democracy. However, it is doubtful whether the section can be seen as being representative of public opinion. Rather, those who write there tend to be persons who feel very strongly about particular issues. This implies a risk of over-representation of views that are more firmly held and more extreme than mainstream ideas. Also, groups with a relatively narrow range of interests tend to dominate the discussion (Wahl-Jorgensen 2004:91). As Wahl-Jorgensen (2004:96) makes clear, letters on the subjects of race, sexuality and religion tend to be both the most numerous and the most emotionally laden. Having said this, the letters page is still indicative of the sentiments and undercurrents that exist in a society. For analytical purposes, however, and also for the sake of any attempts to try to forestall the diffusion and entrenchment of certain dangerous ideas about for example immigration and multiculturalism, it is vital to acquire some indications of the sentiments that are brewing 'out there'. For they certainly influence the wider public in one way or another (cf. Wahl-Jorgensen 2004:91), and it is perhaps more important to ascertain *what* these sentiments are than to engage in the debate on whether the chicken—the newspapers' views—or the egg—the public's views—came first.

Research on Media Stereotypes of Strangers and Risk

In the mid 1970s, Guillaumin (1974:66) noted that stereotypes about race stressed elements of threat and peril, regardless of whether these perils were perceived to be manifested through disease, sexual menace, physical violence or other negative phenomena. In their seminal study of British press, also in the mid 1970s, Hartmann and Husband (1974:163) argued that 'race' seemed to be regarded as a problem that could materialise in different ways, such as through the sheer physical number of immigrants, perceived risks of conflicts and fights following in their wake, or the discrimination and overt hostility which their presence provoked from the majority population. Indeed, contemporary discourses on ethnicity bear a striking resemblance to yesterday's discourses on race (Wigerfelt 2004). Where race used to be an explanatory factor behind worrisome and aberrant behaviour, now culture, strongly associated with ethnicity, seems to have been given that particular role (cf. Lindberg 1998:10).

David Sibley (1995) argues that in majority population discourses, excluded minorities, notably certain ethnic groups, tend in the final analysis to be associated with uncleanliness and filth. Here again, we are reminded of President Putin's blunt statements about his Chechen adversaries. In general, it is not uncommon that a combination of contagious disease and criminality is encountered in Western media reporting about immigrants and refugees (Hier & Greenberg 2002). This is certainly the case, for example, regarding news about the deliberate spreading of HIV infections. One such case was high on the Swedish news agenda a couple of years ago, and it was reported markedly often that the perpetrator was of immigrant origin.

It is imperative to ponder the societal consequences of such negative descriptions, since they can be expected to correspond to and mould prevalent ways of thinking among the public. In her research, Mary Douglas (1992) has helpfully discerned some major types of libel that target marginalised minority groups. In brief, they correspond to the food libel ('foreigners eat disgusting foods'), the sex libel ('foreigners display an aggressive and uncontrolled sexual urge') and, most pointedly, the blood libel ('foreigners pose a lethal danger to us'). The latter kind is clearly the most hazardous one, corresponding quite closely to a discourse on threat, but it may well be combined with the other kinds also. Intuitively, when combinations of all libel types are prevalent in a society, sentiments can easily be set ablaze.

As argued above, news and views about deviant behaviour help to maintain prevalent ideas of what are and what should be the normative boundaries of the majoritarian society. They provide information on what is right and wrong, as well as on the nature of the borderlines which should not be transgressed by decent, well-behaving citizens (Cohen 1987:17). This makes for instance news media reporting on criminal acts an important object of study. As pointed out repeatedly by media analysts, this is a section where references to immigrants abound and do so grossly out of proportion (van Dijk 1987, Brune 2002). If only implicitly, the crime reports provide the normative criteria that are employed in a society and delineates who is inside and who is outside the normative community of the majority. Thus, if we turn to previous research on the stereotypes used to depict immigrants, we find prolific examples indicating that the strangers and the strange encountered therein tend to be associated with crime but also contagious disease and other kinds of danger and menace. This is the 'murder, epidemic and looting' that Bauman (1998:75-76) talks about.

In his critical discourse analyses of Western elite communication about ethnic groups in mass media and other venues, van Dijk (1987:364-366) distilled some typical 'structures of prejudice'. These not only included ideas about the large physical numbers of immigrants, but also about criminality and aggressiveness, the undue competition and affirmative action perceived to create an economic burden on the majority population, as well as ideas about cultural clashes and ascribed personality traits, all of which had the implied inferiority of the immigrated individuals as their common denominator. Attention was very seldom given to positive contributions made by minority groups (van Dijk 1987:365). Van Dijk further (1987:58) generalised these structures of prejudice to encompass any of three prevailing basic themes. Immigrants were either described in terms of difference, deviance or threat. The standard news item would imply that the minorities in question would cause social, economic or political problems for the majority population. In general, stories of crime, threat, aggression and cultural conflict tended to dominate the reports about minorities (van Dijk 1987:361).

In her study of Finnish-Swedish news media coverage of Somali immigrants in Finland, Camilla Haavisto (2002:119) identified two basic stereotypes, namely, 'enemies' and 'victims'. And in a related and preceding study, Nylund (2000:72) found two prevailing themes in Finnish-Swedish press reports about immigrants; namely their forced refugee status and their perceived criminality. Again, they were either depicted as victims or perpetrators. In the Swedish context, Ylva Brune (2002) analysed the media debate on so-called honorary crimes. A common theme was, she argued, that male Muslims were characterised as merciless perpetrators, who were programmed and prompted by their culture to act in a certain manner, whereas Muslim women tended do be described as passive and hapless victims, similarly kept in check by their all-determining culture. Brune observed, for instance, a pattern in Swedish media reports on gang rapes in suburbs. If committed by immigrant men, cultural mores suppressing and denigrating women were described as the determining factors, whereas perpetrators representing the Swedish majority population were instead said to be driven by individual factors, such as mental disorder or the abuse of alcohol or narcotics (Brune 2002; cf. Hylland Eriksen 2001).

'The ethnic is always infantilised in the media', argues Danjoux (2002: 149), adding that it is either depicted as 'tame and endearing' (like in 'ethnic culture', 'ethnic music') or as 'unchained and dangerous' (like in 'ethnic demands' and 'ethnic conflicts'). The effect of these characterisations is that 'the ethnic' becomes represented as something differentiated and clearly separated from the majority 'Us'. The stereotypes which the majority group employs permit it to express its ambivalence towards the 'Others', and thus convey its rejection as well as attraction (Riggins 1997:9). Demonisation and romantisation often go hand in hand (Barany 2002:63-64). Some 30 years ago Guillaumin (1974:79) observed that minorities who are marginalised and excluded are depicted as either above the norm or below it, but rarely described in neutral terms. This description still holds. When members of those categories are described as above the norm, there is reason to fear them, and when they are depicted as below the norm, they can safely be ignored because of their ostensibly crude and uncouth manner or other repellent characteristics.

Stereotypes to Be Expected

So, what patterns of stereotyping should we expect to find in a study on contemporary media coverage on immigrants? We can be rather sure to find expressions of rejection as well as attraction, and representations of the unchained as well as the domesticated. One probable basic stereotype is sure to be one of immigrants as a *risk or threat*, regardless of whether this is manifested through criminality, contagious disease or purportedly aggressive or else deviant cultural practices. A second stereotype which is related, albeit somewhat more moderate, would depict the immigrant as a *burden*, above all in economic terms. When this particular stereotype is employed, the individual will often attain more of the contours of a passive object, and less the ones of an active and menacing subject. The frequent image of the immigrant as a victim will fit in here. S/he will tend to be described as a weak person who needs to be taken care of, and in the final analysis this will amount to her/him being seen as a burden. In the case of both basic stereotypes individual immigrants are portrayed as parts of collectives, where postulated group characteristics are taken to apply to all individual members.

The *exotic stranger* is a third stereotype that we can expect to find. As we have seen, previous research has only very rarely been able to discern positive counter images to the stereotypes denoting threat and burden. And although the exotic might appear rather positive on the surface, it should be kept in mind that it too represents the immature and the irresponsible that, in larger numbers, needs to be taken care of by those wise and adult persons or groups of persons who know better (cf. Hedetoft 1990:46). Hence, the exotic in the end also turns out to constitute a burden. According to this image, the exotic may, if un-chained, grow to dangerous proportions, particularly if it is represented by too many individuals in the very midst of the majority population. Then it easily at-tains the features of a threat.

Despite the overwhelming prevalence of these three basic forms of stereo-type however, let us, for the sake of argument, present a fourth possible stereotype: the immigrant as an *asset*. This would amount to the image that van Dijk found to be so rare in Western news reports. There is no doubt, however, that this image is occasionally encountered. It is familiar within most news con-texts, and the variant that is most proliferated is the individual success story. However, for a set of idealised stereotypes to work as a tool of analysis, the component parts have to possess a certain depth and scope. We need to ask our-selves whether they really amount to stereotyped descriptions of individuals, i.e. whether they represent simplified beliefs about whole categories of people based upon perceived group characteristics, or whether instead they simply boil down to the exceptions that prove the rules. Already at this stage, I would like to stress that the latter will probably hold true for this fourth image of the immigrant as an asset. If it does have a net effect, it is likely merely to entrench negative stereotypes rather than being instrumental in their erosion.

This is so because there is an additional facet to the individual success story that needs to be kept in mind here. 'Virtue has no gossip value', says de Groot (2001). I would concur with this statement, provided that one caveat is added: 'Virtue has no gossip value—if virtue is believed to be the norm'. In the case of the press reporting on immigrants and asylum-seekers in Western Europe, virtue is certainly not believed to be the norm, and its opposite, vice, most notably in the guise of crime, always maintains gossip value. And the main point here is that if vice is considered to be the norm, cases of virtuous conduct by individual immigrants is also believed to be newsworthy. By implication, the individual case of the immigrant do-gooder or the immigrant success story by inference speaks eloquently about the silent majority, thus confirming that as a rule, im-migrants commit criminal acts or, at least, constitute a burden. 'Whiteness' as a normative identity is 'invisible and unmarked' (Train 2000; see also Moon & Nakayama 2005). So is the virtuous behaviour of the normal inhabitant of the majority population. Ethnic and class-related factors tend to go hand in hand in reinforcing marginalisation, and 'middle-class whites become the possessors not of a visible 'culture' but an invisible cultural normalcy' (Tyler 2003:401). 'Whiteness', as normality, is reflected and understood through 'Otherness', which is why reporting on aberrant behaviour is so important as an identity marker. It is important for the majority to know that they are virtuous or at least decent, and it is important to know that there are excluded Others who do not qualify for either label.

As we shall see, the basic stereotypes depicting immigrants as threats or burdens are profusely represented in the news media material featured in this study. The exotic can also be found there, even if it is less frequently encoun-tered in the coverage on the particular local communities under scrutiny. The individual success stories are also to be found, with the double-edged capacity that is their inherent characteristic.

In summary, there is a multitude of risks perceived in the mediated imaginary of contemporary society. Many, if not most, tend to be associated with outgroups, most typically perhaps, immigrants. It is now time to turn to empirical illustrations of this. The following chapters all deal with examples gathered in a Swedish context and concern events that were retold by a local newspaper in the very first years of the 21st century. Lest there be the mistaken belief that these are phenomena that are exclusively to be found in Sweden, however, I will end this chapter by recounting a Danish example of how risk discourse is employed by the majority population to address the issue of immigration. For perceived risks can spill over into alleged dangers and threats, and the Danish case reveals instances when this borderline could very well be said to have been transgressed.

A Danish Illustration

The following sections about a Danish example of the stereotyping of outsiders is primarily included to provide some counterpoints and comparative perspectives to the Swedish illustrations with which the remainder of the book is preoccupied. Danish national politics was, after the elections of 2001, dominated by a change in governmental power whereby a coalition of non-socialist parties took over the helm to form a minority cabinet. It could do so by relying on the parliamentary support of the populist Danish People's Party, which had tipped the scales of the parliamentarian majority. Before and throughout the election campaign of 2001, the party had made itself known as a vehement critic of Danish refugee policy, and questions pertaining to this realm were placed at the very top of the party's political agenda. Evidently, this was a popular move, and it acquired broad support at the polls, rendering it the third largest party in the Danish parliament. Even though the established bourgeois parties refused to accept the party as a fully-fledged member of the cabinet-forming coalition, the party and its leader Pia Kjaersgaard managed to cash in on its restrictive views in exchange for giving the new cabinet its parliamentary support. Thus, the new government soon became associated with restrictive policies on immigration and the reception of refugees. To mention but a few aspects of this new turn in government policy, daily allowances to asylum-seekers were slashed radically, reunifications of refugee families were to be subjected to restrictive scrutiny, the granting of political asylum became decidedly less generous, the minimum stay required to obtain permanent residence permits was extended to seven years, severe restrictions were put on Danish citizens intending to marry foreigners and settle in Denmark, and the tuition and grants to education in home languages were drastically cut.

In this chapter, we shall see how the unfolding political drama at the national level in Denmark was reflected in a local context during the year of 2002. The setting chosen is the town of Skive, situated in the northern part of the Jutland peninsula. The town itself has some 21 000 inhabitants, and we shall approach it through its local newspaper, *Skive Folkeblad*. The paper is a highly localised one that only covers Skive itself as well as the neighbouring municipalities of Sundsøre, Sallingsund, Spøttrup, Fjends and Vinderup (cf. Nordahl Svendsen 1979). It has an overall daily circulation of about 13 000 copies. The second page of the paper is an op-ed forum where editorials are published alongside articles of debate and letters-to-the-editor. The local news quite tangibly predominate the paper, and on its homepage it is made clear that this is the image that it really wishes to convey (www.skivefolkeblad.dk, accessed on 11 August 2003).

Because of its integrated op-ed page, *Skive Folkeblad* has a forum where national politics can in a natural manner be transformed onto the local format. During 2002, profuse attention was given to immigration and refugee policies. It almost seemed to be a daily preoccupation to publish articles on these matters, and we shall now turn to the essence of the articles published during the year. Since the op-ed page was an integrated one, borders were at times confused between what constituted debating articles and what constituted letters-to-the-editor, which probably resulted in giving the latter a higher status than they otherwise would have had.

Stigmatisation of Muslims

With notable frequency, *Skive Folkeblad* singled out Muslims as a collective. The prevalent tone was harsh and negative, and Muslims as a group were often depicted as risks and threats to core values of the Danish nation. This was clearly a reflection of what was already a prominent discourse pursued at the national level. One author of an article in the debate section, for example, held that 'Muslims who read the Quran in a fundamentalist way are almost impossible to integrate into the Danish society' (*Skive Folkeblad* 11-12 May 2002, p. 9). Another voice queried when it would become the 'will of Allah' that the Islamic movement gained governmental power in Denmark (*Skive Folkeblad* 21 June 2002, p. 2). Yet another writer believed it to be 'impossible' to mix Islam and the 'Christian values prevalent in the so far democratic state of Denmark' (*Skive Folkeblad* 10 July 2002, p. 2). In short, Islamic fundamentalism—perceived as the sole representative of the Islamic religion as a whole—was claimed to have the potential to devastate and destroy democracy in Denmark at its very roots. Spelling out this argument, one writer of a letter-to-the-editor feared that a total destruction of democracy might be the result in a future where Muslims were to gain the majority of the Danish population as they would, it was argued, thus find themselves in a position to introduce *sharia* laws into Danish legislation (*Skive Folkeblad* 5 August 2002, p. 2). A representative of the Danish People's Party proposed that all Islamic fundamentalists who resided in Denmark should be subjected to a careful head count so as to give the authorities a basis for assessing the extent of 'subversive activities' performed in the country (*Skive Folkeblad* 8 August 2002, p. 2).

On another occasion, an imam who was active in Denmark was given the floor. This might, at first glance, appear to be an effort to provide some space for countervailing opinions and thus influences on the readers. However, what the imam did was to defend an internationally much debated court case, where a woman in Nigeria had been sentenced to be stoned to death for adultery. The imam went as far as expressing his view that 'stoning is all right'. Even though it is a very cruel punishment, he claimed, Allah had decreed the punishment in order to prevent humans from 'committing adultery' (*Skive Folkeblad* 20-21 April 2002, p. 2). Certainly, the imam's words were likely to confirm the views of those readers who were already prejudiced toward Muslims and the practice of their religion, and may very well have converted many more to such views besides. The responsibility for selecting the voices to represent Muslims and give them the rostrum, however, was plainly that of the editors and in this case they clearly did not select a representative of any Muslim majority.

To be fair, potentially dissenting or at least moderating voices were on some occasions given the opportunity to speak. Nonetheless, such voices of relative moderation represented a minority of the total number of articles published, and they certainly conveyed stories of at least highly influential and radical Muslim minorities.

During the year under study, there were several sub-discussions within the broader theme of Islam as a perceived threat. One of them surfaced in connection with a proposal from the military supreme command regarding how integration best be furthered within the Danish national defence. To this end, it was suggested that it be permitted for soldiers and officers to observe religious rituals during working hours. One writer of a letter-to-the-editor confessed to be 'deeply shaken' by the fact that Denmark was so 'infected by Muslim traditions' that the armed forces would have to wait for those soldiers who had to say their prayers first before they could perform their duties (*Skive Folkeblad* 9 July 2002 p. 2). The choice of wording should be especially noted here; Islam is an 'infection', and thus considered to be a disease that has to be countered in order that Danish public health be preserved.

Another letter-writer spoke vividly about the risk of acquiring a fifth column within the country. According to him, soldiers could now enter the military in spite of them having 'a totally unreliable and lethally dangerous' sense of loyalty (*Skive Folkeblad* 19 July 2002, p. 2). The colonel commanding the military barracks at Skive—which is one of the biggest military establishments in Denmark—was also not very happy about the proposal put forward by the defence command. According to him, ethnic minorities had so far posed no problem at the barracks. Rather, he held, the Danish defence was 'good at integrating' people from different backgrounds. Now, however, he feared that the proposal would provide 'the notorious immigrants-haters with more rifle munition' (*Skive Folkeblad* 15 July 2002, p. 4).

Another sub-discussion on the theme of Islam as a threat took place towards the end of the year. The catalyst was a government proposal that it be made mandatory for medical officers serving at Danish compulsory schools to report encountered cases of genital mutilation among female pupils. On the basis of such reports, parents or others championing the abusive surgery could then be prosecuted by law. In Skive, however, the head medical officer of the municipal schools wrote an article in *Skive Folkeblad* arguing that he personally did not intend to fulfil the new obligation. If the authorities had their way and made him act as a 'supervisory agency', he believed he would lose the entire confidence he enjoyed from the immigrant parents. They would probably cease to send their children to him for observation and treatment altogether. Thus, he would not get the opportunity to treat grave diseases that the children might carry, such as tuberculosis (*Skive Folkeblad* 14 November 2002, p. 3).

There was a markedly negative response to the doctor's article. Among the more modest speakers in the debate was a local politician who criticised him for failing to fulfil his duties (*Skive Folkeblad* 15 November 2002, p. 1). Another letter-writer blamed him for being so 'afraid of conflicts' so as to be 'irresponsible'. That writer went on to suggest that all young women be subjected to mandatory examinations once a year and that those doctors who failed to report encountered cases of genital mutilation of women to the authorities be punished for their shortcomings (*Skive Folkeblad* 16-17 November 2002). The doctor should be ashamed of himself for his views, another writer held (*Skive Folkeblad* 19 November 2002, p. 2). As a further facet to the discussion, it was argued that those 'uneducated Somalis' who did not wish to understand Danish legislation should either start to live by it or else, if they continued to practise genital mutilation of women, they should quite simply be forced to leave the country (*Skive Folkeblad* 18 November 2002, p. 2).

Clearly put on the defensive, the medical officer re-entered the debate. Circumcision of women was a 'hideous operation' which should be abolished as soon as possible, he explained. He assured the readers that he had personally never been against the idea of reporting the abuses, but what he objected to was the notion of 'going after and punishing the parents' rather than 'helping the Somali girls'. The newly established national government, which had launched the proposal about the mandatory reports, was a xenophobic one, he argued (*Skive Folkeblad* 3 December 2002, p. 3). He articulated his views emphatically but his perspective clearly amounted to a minority position in the local debate.

Children at Risk: Preschool and Hepatitis

It was, however, another debate that really set the emotions of the readers of *Skive Folkeblad* ablaze. Again, the discussion touched upon themes such as doctors, health services, children and refugees. At its heart was the issue of immigrants who had been found to carry a contagious disease, and who thus were seen as posing grave threats to public health, not least among children.

Already in the early spring there had been an article in *Skive Folkeblad* stating that cases of Hepatitis B had been encountered in the municipalities of Skive and Fjends. It had come to the knowledge of the newspaper that refugee children were carriers and that the disease could be lethal for those who had not been vaccinated against it. Contagion could be transmitted through cuts and bruises, even if the risk as a rule was deemed to be low. The district medical officer argued that everything was 'under complete control' and that no-one needed to worry about contagion (*Skive Folkeblad* 7 March 2002, p. 4). The continuation of the story, however, showed that no heed was paid to the doctor's reassuring remarks.

On the contrary, there was from June onwards a long series of articles about two small refugee children in the village of Stoholm (in the municipality of Fjends) who both had contracted Hepatitis B. The real crux of the matter was that the children were to start attending a preschool in Stoholm after the summer vacation and an intense debate unfolded around this theme. The parents of Danish majority children were quick and plentiful in voicing their anger and frustration (*Skive Folkeblad* 7 June 2002, p. 2; 10 June 2002, p. 3; 21 June 2002, p. 7; 28 June 2002, p. 4; 4 July 2002, p. 2; 22 August 2002, p. 4; 26 August 2002, p. 2 . 8; 28 August 2002, p. 2). The doctor continued to assure the readership that the risk for contagion was low, but to be on the safe side he recommended that all children be vaccinated (*Skive Folkeblad* 10 June p.3; 21 June 2002, p. 7; 28 June 2002, p. 4; 4 July 2002, p. 2). This could be construed as rather contradictory statements, and were probably not very successful in calming down the upset public.

Next in the chain of events, 30 parents signed a petition where they demanded that the two children would not be received at preschool until six months later. The basic idea was that the period of quarantine would grant the parents of the other children sufficient time to be confident that the vaccine had started to work (*Skive Folkeblad* 28 June 2002, p. 4). Incidentally, the populist Danish People's Party, trying to exploit the situation to its advantage, announced its support for the petitioning parents (*Skive Folkeblad* 21 June 2002, p. 7). Still, the politicians of the municipality of Fjends decided to stand by their decision to admit the two children to preschool. 'Our point is that the integration of the refugee children is vital', said the chairman of the Committee for children and culture issues (*Skive Folkeblad* 4 July 2002, p. 2).

In August, when the preschool had resumed its activities after the summer break, the debate started anew. One letter-writer, who was markedly upset, recounted that a 'Danish' child had been bitten 'by a refugee child contagious with Hepatitis' (*Skive Folkeblad* 22 August 2002, p. 4). The imagery was very vivid and the frontlines between the majority Us and the minority Them emerged clearly on the pages of the newspaper. The district medical officer took the floor soon afterwards, reassuring that the risk for contagion for the bitten child was so small as to be 'non-existent'. In concluding, he stressed that he henceforth intended not to make any more statements on the issue, since he believed it to be vital to give the preschool personnel time to concentrate on their activities (*Skive Folkeblad* 22 August 2002, p. 4). Others, however, did not share this view.

One writer argued that the way the politicians had handled the issue was counter-productive. Instead of promoting the integration of the refugees, which was probably the original intention, he argued, it risked contributing to their isolation from society. To his mind, there was a risk that the local inhabitants would unleash their frustration with the politicians and take it out on the refugees (*Skive Folkeblad* 26 August 2002, p. 2). Furthermore, one infuriated parent argued that the preschool teachers had started to harass children of critically-minded parents. His family had therefore decided to sell their house and move on to another municipality. If they turned out to be unable to sell the house, the letter-writer concluded, he believed that they could 'rent it to the municipality that can pass it on to those refugees whom it treats so well' (*Skive Folkeblad* 28 August 2002, p. 2). Someone also argued that what was going on was in essence 'discrimination in reverse' (*Skive Folkeblad* 26 August 2002, p. 2).

These were clearly the most dramatic tidings reported on by the Danish local newspaper during 2002. Evidently there was ample use of risk discourse here, and on several occasions it seemed to go over the top, evolving into a fully-fledged threat discourse about imminent danger. Preventive action was undertaken on a collective scale among the settled majority, especially as the 'Danish children' were allegedly subjected to contagious illness from (the Muslim) abroad.

Setting the Scene for the Swedish Cases: Facts about *Smålänningen*

With these statements the Danish illustration ends. It is now time to deal, somewhat more at length, with what the Swedish local newspaper *Smålänningen* discussed in relation to its three municipalities of coverage and distribution: Ljungby, Markaryd and Älmhult. I shall commence with the most dramatic example, Markaryd. All three examples have something to say about the way risk discourse is used by the mouthpiece of the majority population and how stories about socio-cultural risk are narrated in different ways.

Before I analyse the chains of events and discussions that took place in these municipalities during the course of this study, some words are due about the newspaper itself. *Smålänningen* is a markedly local newspaper and has no aspirations to be more than that. With its circulation of some 13 200 copies a day, it belongs to the so-called Herenco sphere of daily newspapers in Sweden.[1] The paper covers three municipalities in the province of Småland in southern Sweden: Markaryd, Ljungby (which is its absolute stronghold), and Älmhult. Indeed, its coverage of households in two of the municipalities is impressive: 70.5 per cent in Ljungby, 60 per cent in Markaryd and 31 per cent in Älmhult. According to the newspaper's own estimations, 88 per cent of all inhabitants in Ljungby will read the paper during an average day (interview Davidsson, Gustavsson). It is, in other words, a very influential actor in the local community.

Since somewhere in the early 1980s, the editorials of *Smålänningen* have been written centrally at the Liberal News Agency in Stockholm. There was an obvious effect emanating from this, namely that the editorials dealt with matters that were relevant from a national centre perspective, but that were decidedly less so locally. This gave rise to some frustration among the local journalists, as they felt deprived of the chance to use the editorials to comment on current local political affairs. In order to balance this deficit a little, the second page of the paper contained a debate section, to which the editors tried to attract representatives of the local political elite (interviews with Gustafsson and Davidsson). There were also other ways of compensating for the absence of editorial columns written locally. The letters-to-the-editor section became more important than it most likely would have been otherwise.

According to the editors, all readers were not fully aware of the fact that the editorials were not written in Ljungby but were instead dispatched from the national capital. However, to the extent that it was known to the readers, it would certainly tend to exacerbate the trend among them to, at the expense of the editorials, prioritise local news when reading the paper. This general trend of which pages were prioritised was corroborated by the media consumption studies performed by *Smålänningen* itself. Whereas, for example, the local pages devoted to Ljungby were read in their entirety or almost in their entirety by 52 per cent of the readers, the editorials were given a very low ranking. Only 22 per cent of the readers claimed to read them in their entirety or almost in their entirety (material provided by Idofson).

Polls conducted by *Smålänningen* itself show the letters-to-the editor section to be one of the most widely read sections in the paper. While the family-related pages were the most popular by far (76 per cent), the letters-to-the-editor section also scored highly among the sections and ended up in third position (54 per cent), barely distanced by the pages devoted to radio and television (56 per cent). This made the letters section even more popular than the news pages devoted to the newspaper's stronghold, Ljungby (material provided by Idofson). It is therefore quite reasonable to assume that letters addressed to the editor have quite some impact on the audience, even though the readers may not directly sympathise with all the views expressed therein. I will therefore devote considerable attention to this section of the paper in the chapter on Ljungby. First, however, events in the nearby municipality of Markaryd will be dealt with.

Notes

1. This conglomeration consists of a number of regional newspapers in Småland and Västergötland, with *Jönköpingsposten* as the single largest daily.

5. The Power of Stereotypes: Asylum-seekers in Markaryd

This is a story about the municipality of Markaryd in southern Sweden and how the encounters between the settled majority and the asylum-seekers received there were reported by the local newspaper *Smålänningen* during the year 2002. Indeed, of the local Swedish examples presented in this book, Markaryd provides the most drastic and pointed one. Here, risk discourse had most of the time already been transposed into more heated modes of talk and argumentation. For according to the news pages of the local daily, it was rather a matter of imminent danger and threat that was looming over the town. These threats were allegedly posed by asylum-seekers who had been received in unexpectedly high numbers during the first months of the year. According to the press reports and the societal moods reflected in them, the asylum-seekers were responsible for a large increase in crimes committed in Markaryd. This mainly concerned shoplifting and thefts, but judging from the highly concerned discussions on the ground, societal values were also certainly seen to be at bay.

Judged also by Swedish national standards, this is a rather extreme story about the relations between the settled majority and immigrant groups. My aim with this chapter is not to undertake any finger-pointing in the direction of Markaryd and its inhabitants. I do not intend it to be an exercise in naming and shaming. Rather, my point is to say that even if the societal discussion was quite inflamed, the underlying argumentation was based on stereotypes that were informed by tenets of what could be called banal localism and indeed racism. These, in turn, display a sadly universal calibre. My argument is therefore simply that, given a similar mix of contextual factors and triggers, Markaryd could be located and could materialise anywhere in Sweden or indeed in the Western world. I could equally well have chosen to nickname the community of study, as both Katharine Tyler (2003) and Karin Norman (2004) elegantly have done. I have, however, refrained from doing so, not because it is important to underline that these events took place in Markaryd, Sweden, but rather to stress that they have taken place, full stop. In other words, the events are not fictitious.

The characterisation of a Markaryd beset by severe crisis due to the presence of a large number of asylum-seekers was brought home by the newspaper reporting in *Smålänningen*. Political actors of the municipality were given the opportunity to deliver their messages about the negative impact of the asylum-seekers on its pages, but precious few representatives of the asylum-seekers themselves were given the chance to articulate counter-stories. The fact is that the message was mainly delivered by the news pages of the paper. This is noteworthy, as it again indicates that the old sub-division into objective news stories and subjective editorials is indeed a dated one. The selection of news and angles matters and could even be said to be all important.

The Story in Brief: The Reception of Asylum-seekers

With its fewer than 10 000 inhabitants, Markaryd ranks among the less populated municipalities of Sweden. According to official statistics for the year 2000, 10% of the inhabitants were born abroad, which was somewhat below the national average. There are no permanent facilities for receiving asylum-seekers in Markaryd, but from time to time a temporary compound has been in active use. The physical numbers received there have experienced noticeable swings. There was a peak in the early 1990s in connection with the wars in former Yugoslavia, whereas there was a notable downturn towards the end of the decade. By way of indication, the municipality received a mere 4 asylum-seekers in 1999 (*Välfärdsdata Kronobergs län* 2000).

In 2002 there was a crest. Having been closed down for 18 months, the reception facilities in Markaryd were reopened in January. By March around 350 had arrived. Of these, most were housed in Markaryd itself, while 150 were located in another village, Strömsnäsbruk, in the same municipality. Most of those arriving in the first round came from the former Soviet Union, Mongolia, Turkey, Albania and the former Yugoslavia (*Smålänningen* 8 January 2002, p. 11; 12 April 2002, p. 15).

The municipal authorities were later to be harsh in their criticism of the Swedish Migration Board, arguing that the Board had failed to inform them about the expected size of the influx (*Smålänningen* 5 September 2002, p. 12). It had negotiated directly and exclusively with the privately owned municipal housing company, which had had plenty of available housing space, and had not deemed it necessary to inform the municipal authorities about what was in the offing.

An Increase in Minor Crime

In early January 2002 *Smålänningen* reported a notable increase in shoplifting incidents in Markaryd. There was a simultaneous rise in burglaries targeting private houses. A newly appointed municipal commissioner, representing the Social Democrats, was quick to make a statement about the situation. He observed that there had been seven shoplifting incidents reported to the police during one single week in January, and even though this was in itself a modest figure, it was as many as there had been during the whole year before. Apparently, asylum-seekers had been implicated in several of the incidents. The commissioner's conclusion was rash. Perpetrators of crime, even petty ones, should be evicted from the country without further ado. The inquiry into their rights of gaining asylum protection in Sweden should be aborted at once, he remarked (*Smålänningen* 16 January 2002, p. 10).

Most leading politicians in Markaryd were more cautious and refrained from openly backing the commissioner's statements. One exception at that point was a representative of a local populist party called the Alternative, who agreed that asylum-seekers should automatically be evicted if they committed any kind of offence, such as shoplifting, during the time of inquiry (*Smålänningen* 17 January 2002, p. 10). Another locally prominent politician, representing the Christian Democrats, also backed the essence of the commissioner's diagnosis, stating his disappointment that 'here they come as guests to a country which generously opens up its borders for them, and then they use this confidence in this manner' (*Smålänningen* 16 January 2002, p. 10). The 'guest' metaphor connotes quite a restrictive view of the right to asylum. Guests eat and drink for free, but they should know their place, be respectful to their hosts—and if caught misbehaving, it is legitimate to evict them from the premises.

Several voices spoke out among the public in favour of the commissioner's suggestion. Anyone displaying a 'criminal disposition', should be sent back immediately, according to a writer of a letter-to-the-editor (*Smålänningen* 17 January 2002, p. 10). Local traders similarly backed the municipal commissioner's ideas: 'We are quite a few who support [the Social Democratic commissioner], but everybody is afraid of being branded as a racist', remarked a shopkeeper, who wished to remain anonymous (*Smålänningen* 29 January 2002, p. 13).

Together with the staff at the reception compound, the regional representatives of the Swedish Migration Board tried to respond to the discontent. To this end, they indicated the possibility that inquiry times be shortened for people who had committed serious offences while staying in Sweden. They did not think, however, that cases of shoplifting belonged to that category. A local director of the Migration Board made the estimate that, among the about 350 asylum-seekers in Markaryd, only 5-10 might be suspected of having a criminal record (*Smålänningen* 8 February 2002, p. 14).

In the meantime, the number of shoplifting incidents and burglaries continued to soar. Commenting on the development, the other municipal commissioner of Markaryd, who represented the Christian Democrats, remarked: 'These burglaries are a tragic fact, and of course we do suspect that they have something to do with our guests here in the municipality. But I do believe that even the Swedes make use of the situation [with under-staffing and low accessibility of the police]' (*Smålänningen* 20 February 2002, p. 12).

This statement was interesting and is worth dwelling upon for several reasons. First of all, the guest metaphor was invoked again. The commissioner's subdivision of the inhabitants of Markaryd into 'Swedes' and 'guests' was also very telling. There were evidently no overlaps between the two categories; inhabitants belonged to either of them, never to both simultaneously. The impression was indeed that never the twain shall meet. His use of the words 'of course' was revealing as well. By using the phrase he seemed to refer to self-evidence and facts beyond dispute, where there indeed was nothing of the kind. Furthermore, the commissioner's disclaimer that 'even Swedes' might be among those committing the crimes connoted that this constituted an exception to the rule. The conclusion was that the asylum-seekers were the chief offenders.

Even so, it did seem at the time as if this commissioner's analysis was indicative in many respects of local sentiments in Markaryd; quite clearly, the public was alarmed. Disabled people were among those who voiced their concern most (*Smålänningen* 20 February 2002, p. 12). Parents were also afraid to leave their children at home on their own (*Smålänningen,* 6 March 2002, p. 15).

According to the impression conveyed by *Smålänningen,* the community was sizzling with rumours. Matters came to a head in mid-April, when an armed robbery occurred in central Markaryd, in which a local taxi owner was assaulted by a man speaking in 'broken Swedish' (*Smålänningen* 11 April 2002, p. 15). The newspaper also reported on several incidents at the reception facilities themselves. One asylum-seeker was threatened with a knife by another refugee after having tried to talk the wrongdoer out of occupying himself with stealing and hoarding (*Smålänningen* 11 April 2002, p. 4). A woman reported that she had been raped by two fellow male asylum-seekers (*Smålänningen* 28 March 2002, p. 15). And in early May one worried asylum-seeker spoke to a journalist at *Smålänningen,* explaining that he felt wrongly accused together with most other inmates at the camp. He desired to work and make himself useful. But, he conceded, 'I know that there are sex criminals as well as thieves among the asylum-seekers' (*Smålänningen* 7 May 2002, p. 13). For those in the community who sought confirmation of their views that the reception facilities constituted a den of criminal offenders, this voice could certainly be construed as providing corroboration. The impression was rather that his was an isolated voice belonging to the category of decent people who, albeit perhaps a majority in numbers, were fairly irrelevant in affecting overall developments.

The Community Responds

The inhabitants of the local community did not sit idly by, waiting to become victims of new thefts and burglaries. If there was to be any kind of confrontation between the settled majority and the stigmatised group of asylum-seekers, the former seemed poised to take it on.

Several local strategies were formulated to counter the perceived threat. For example, neighbourhood action networks were established and organised to prevent and forestall burglaries of private homes. During the first six months of the year, 13 such groups had seen the light of day (*Smålänningen* 13 June 2002, p. 14). The groups were said to be a 'good way to keep the thieves away from the door' (*Smålänningen* 14 June 2002, p. 29), and the secretary of the local council for crime prevention argued that they were actually very efficient in keeping the rate of criminality down (*Smålänningen* 5 December 2002, p. 12). Individuals willing to join such networks of community action received stickers to put on their doors, and neighbours kept watch for each other. In case of suspect-looking cars or individuals being sighted in the area, the members alerted each other by phone (*Smålänningen* 10 October 2002, p. 9). However, there seemed to be a discernible risk that these initiatives would turn into vigilante networks, and on one occasion the police informed people willing to get organised in neighbourhood community action that 'violence might be legitimate, but you do not have the right to knock anyone down' (*Smålänningen* 27 February 2002, p. 13). By giving such instructions the police seemed to be balancing on a tightrope indeed.

The local traders convened and drew up a six-point programme that they presented to the municipal authorities. The first point was draconian, as it stipulated that all asylum-seekers should be forced to stay indoors between 7 am and 5 pm, and that they should be kept busy during these hours in different compulsory activities. 'All of us have to work, so we think it is proper that those who come here will have to do so as well', the chairman of the local committee for crime prevention said (*Smålänningen* 28 February 2002, p. 12). 'They are parasites using our welfare system without having to do anything in return. They should be kept in compulsory activity programmes eight hours a day', he later remarked and continued, 'I get annoyed as I go to work every day and see groups of relatively well dressed asylum-seekers just drifting around' (*Smålänningen* 25 April 2002, p. 11).

It is not the case that there was not any counterevidence speaking in favour of the asylum-seekers. There was indeed but, judging by the newspaper coverage, societal reaction to these indices just underlined the resilience of negative stereotypes. Thus, it seemed to be of no avail that representatives of the regional police pointed out that the crime statistics could be questioned, and that the total amount of reported crimes had actually decreased since the corresponding six-month period a year before. Even more importantly, it also did not seem to make any difference that the police authorities in March reported that six people had been apprehended by the police for a series of burglaries of private homes in Markaryd, and that all of these happened to be 'native Swedes' (*Smålänningen* 5 March 2002, p. 19; 8 March 2002, p. 14; 19 March 2002, p. 4; 10 April 2002, p. 7). Rather, things were back where they had started, when a representative of the police conceded that the shoplifting incidents could in their entirety be attributed to asylum-seekers (*Smålänningen* 8 March 2002, p. 14). The overall impression of the local discussion was that it was the latter piece of information that caught on in the public mind. According to the skewed logic of stereotyping, all criminality was attributed to the asylum-seekers, even though only a fraction of them had been implicated in the crimes and apparently the most minor variety at that, namely the shoplifting and not the burglaries.

In the poisoned atmosphere that characterised events in the municipality of Markaryd, more manifest and physical conflicts could be expected. And, indeed, in early April there was a violent incident as Swedish teenagers started a street fight with immigrant youths in central Strömsnäsbruk. What started out as a minor clash rapidly developed into an all-out fight, which ended with assault charges and police action, as patrol cars from Ljungby and the Scanian regional centre of Kristianstad were called to the scene. According to the news reports, the fight had erupted as two teenage immigrants were pushed off their bicycles by 'Swedish' attackers. The single most violent act took place as a 'Swedish' 18-year old rioter beat an antagonist over his chest with an iron bar (*Smålänningen* 4 April 2002, p. 1).

Even though it is of course hard to prove this in a conclusive manner, it seemed as though the general climate of suspicion had prompted this outburst of violence. The front page headline of the article recording the event did little to allay upset feelings: 'Swedes and Immigrants in Street Fight'. If there ever was a clear-cut example of subdividing the world into Us and Them, this was certainly it. In view of media analysts' findings that large categories of readers only take in headlines and snapshots (Pettersson 2003:71-72), the choice of such formulations is highly portentous. Even in cases where the body of the text tells another or at least slightly more nuanced story (which it hardly did in this particular instance), it will be the headline that creates the lasting impression. The rest will simply most often not be read. Thus, the underlying discourse that inspired the formulation of the headline says more and conveys more information than the actual and manifest contents of the article itself (Pettersson 2003:61). 'Swedes' and 'immigrants' were here pitted against one another and, according to the impression created thereby, one cannot belong to both categories at the same time. 'Swedishness' thus connotes invisible normalcy, while belonging to the immigrant category is associated with deviations of some sort, a general failure to conform to cherished and largely taken-for-granted norms (Borevi & Strömblad 2004:10-11). The suggested setting was such that, at the very least, there seemed to be a latent risk for renewed clashes between the groups.

Criminals in the Community Midst

Even if the most inflamed part of the discussions in Markaryd took place during the spring, events did not die down later on in the year. Keen attention continued to be paid to the issue of criminality. The focus on the increased crime rate was steadfastly held on to. There were several reports about this. Whereas the annual average in Markaryd in previous years was 750 reported crimes, in June 2002 a number of 617 had already been reported to the police. For the most part the crimes concerned thefts, but the rate of physical assaults had also soared. In Strömsnäsbruk, 22 crimes had been reported during the first six months, whereas the corresponding figure had been 4 in the previous year. The increase was described by *Smålänningen* as 'extreme' (*Smålänningen* 14 June 2002, p. 29).

At the year's end, a 30-per cent increase had been established as compared to the figures of the year before. The increase primarily pertained to burglaries, thefts and robberies (*Smålänningen* 5 December 2002, p. 12). According to the news reports, the increased reception of asylum-seekers was widely held to be a primary factor accounting for the rising crime rate. Even if the secretary of the local council for crime prevention was more low-key in his assessment than his chairman, who had suggested the six-point programme for combating crime, had been earlier, the main thrust of his diagnosis was clear. The council, he said, had 'not analysed what had caused the increases in the different kinds of crime, but we believe that they partly have to do with the asylum-seekers' (*Smålänningen* 5 December 2002, p. 12).

According to the editors of *Smålänningen*, the policy of the paper is very clear regarding the reporting of crimes implicating immigrants. It does not publish any details about the specific origin or ethnicity of a perpetrator, unless particularly warranted by the case, and unless such a piece of information is believed to add something to the analysis and understanding of the situation (interview Davidson). And indeed, in the Markaryd case, nothing was said about the assumed *specific* ethnicity of the shoplifters; they were just identified as asylum-seekers and/or refugees. This kind of information was, on the other hand, quite often stressed. In not pinpointing any particular ethnic group, the local newspaper was more conscientious than some large national and regional newspapers had been. In connection with a widely publicised event during the summer of 2002 which featured a large-scale and violent beach fight in Ryd, another small-town community in Småland, involving groups of asylum-seekers, these other papers had no qualms about identifying the wrongdoers as being of Roma origin (*Dagens Nyheter* 12 June 2002, *Sydsvenska Dagbladet* 7 June 2002). However, even though the restrictive practices of *Smålänningen* seemed commendable, the flipside of the coin was clearly to bring misdemeanour to the whole group of asylum-seekers. Both strategies have their distinct drawbacks. There is no clear-cut answer to the question how cases like these should be handled, but one can of course question whether it was really necessary to underline the perpetrators' status as asylum-seekers in the first place.

For *Smålänningen* was actually quite prolific in terms of providing the information that certain perpetrators, often of minor crimes, were precisely asylum-seekers. The offences were often so petty as to have a slightly pathetic touch, but they were nonetheless probably prone to heighten the impression among the settled majority that it was subject to heightened risks, and maybe even imminent and actual threat and danger. To cite some examples of the cases that were reported, one asylum-seeker was caught by the police as he tried to steal aluminium-rimmed wheels from a parked car (*Smålänningen* 13 June 2002,

p. 40; 17 June 2002, p. 8). Two other asylum-seekers were apprehended after breaking in at the village dump in Strömsnäsbruk (*Smålänningen* 5 September 2002, p. 4). Another asylum-seeker from Markaryd was reported to have been evicted after having stolen clothes in the capital city Stockholm (*Smålänningen* 11 September 2002, p. 7), while yet another was apprehended while trying to steal a stereo from a car in the neighbourhood (*Smålänningen* 10 October 2002, p. 13). One report claimed that someone had managed to connect their phone to the line of a phone kiosk in Markaryd and use it to make calls to Russia and Belorussia to a value of 1500 Swedish kronor. Nothing was said about the identity of any suspect for this offence, but the readers were free to draw their own conclusions based on the hints available (*Smålänningen* 21 October 2002, p. 8).

On another occasion, the perpetrator was downright ridiculed. Just before Christmas, *Smålänningen* ran a story about an asylum-seeker who had been caught while trying to steal clothes from a tailor's shop in Markaryd. He had simply walked into a fitting booth, put the new clothes on, then put his own clothes on top of them and tried to walk out of the store. When apprehended, he had allegedly claimed that a friend at a reception centre in a nearby municipality had assured him that, in the run-up to Christmas, everyone in Sweden had the right to walk into any shop and grab whatever s/he wanted without paying for it. Everybody did this, the 'friend' had said, and the man had believed him. The headline said: 'Unexpected visit to shop in Markaryd: Christmas clothes were not for free...' (*Smålänningen* 18 December 2002, p. 36). So, according to this particular story, which could easily have posed as an urban legend (see Chapter 7), this token asylum-seeker was not only criminally minded, but was also pretty stupid. Behind it all, the lingering power of negative stereotyping can again be discerned.

Stories such as these all contributed to creating a picture of Markaryd as being beset by asylum-seekers from the reception centre who committed all sorts of crime and brought the society into a stage approaching anarchy. In this there was a striking similarity to Stanley Cohen's (1987) familiar concept 'moral panics'. As made evident by the examples above, they were for the most part trifle stories, but they were numerous and almost certain to leave an impression.

A Visit from the Capital

Not all of the news items concerned minor crimes, however. Towards the end of the summer, there was one item in particular that served to entrench local views that the refugee reception centre was a negative phenomenon and that the asylum-seekers constituted an onus for the community. In late August, the news broke that an 18-year old Russian-speaking woman, believed to be of Estonian origin, had been apprehended staying at the refugee reception centre without a permit. Apparently, she had been smuggled into the reception centre by a male acquaintance, who intended to channel her on to prostitution and trafficking networks in Sweden. To make matters even worse, the woman was caught carrying heroin in her handbag. The intended pimp was himself an asylum-seeker residing at the centre under a false identity (*Smålänningen* 30 August 2002). So, all of a sudden, the worst fears of the local community had seemed to come true. Through the refugee reception centre, it could be claimed, drugs and prostitution had entered into the midst of the gentle local folks.

At much the same time, the then Swedish minister for migration issues, Jan O. Karlsson, paid a visit to Markaryd. He was acting on an invitation issued earlier during the spring by the municipal council for crime prevention, who had wished him to come and 'encounter the problems in the real world' (*Smålänningen* 3 May 2002, p. 13). The meeting between the minister and the council turned out to be heated and turbulent. Among the issues that featured in the debate were questions about the risks for eruptions of racism due to what had taken place in the community. The minister argued that the municipal authorities had to work closely together with the regional branch of the Migration Board as well as with the police, the business community and other public actors. There was a need to ask the question 'what we can do together', he argued. 'As long as one is upset by and reacts to actual events, there is no racism, but the risk emerges as soon as one starts to draw general conclusions despite the lack of corroborating evidence' (*Smålänningen* 2 September 2002, p. 14).

At the meeting, the minister found himself assuming a defensive position. He asserted his view that asylum-seekers implicated in organised crime should be evicted at once. Even so, his statements did not do much to placate the assembled public. The air grew tense as the minister was confronted with the views and concerns of the villagers about the rising rate of criminality and the news reports about trafficking and drug dealing at the reception centre. Mr. Karlsson expressed his dismay about the events. However, his concern was apparently not enough to appease the public. Instead, his audience became more and more adamant. The minister also repeatedly lost his temper, which hardly improved the atmosphere (*Smålänningen* 2 September 2002, p. 14; 3 September 2002, p. 25).

The municipal commissioner representing the Christian Democrats said afterwards that many of those assembled felt disappointed after the meeting. The minister had had nothing concrete to offer; he had just been talking. Someone confessed to having felt like a 'misbehaving poor cousin from the countryside' (*Smålänningen* 3 September 2002, p. 25). The other municipal commissioner, the Social Democrat, remarked: 'The members of the council for crime prevention kept asking the same question over and over again. The minister answered as best as he could, but in the end he was livid'. The commissioner shared the rather general impression that the minister had been 'angry and rude' (*Smålänningen*, 4 September 2002).

Electioneering and the Local Onus

In the ensuing local debate, there was a widening rift between the Social Democratic and the Christian Democratic commissioner, as the latter criticised the former for having agreed with the minister's expressed position that more municipal funds ought to be spent on the integration of the asylum-seekers into local society. The Christian Democrat argued that such activities had to be funded by the state. In the days that followed, the two commissioners had a heated exchange of views about who was to be trusted and who had really wavered from his original line and when. The Christian Democrat implied that his colleague from the Social Democrats was on the verge of backing away from his previously tough stance on crime-committing asylum-seekers (*Smålänningen* 3 & 4 September 2002). His criticism was scathing: 'It is easy for [the Social Democratic commissioner] to play it tough in the local debate, but now he shows once again that he has difficulties representing the interests of the municipality of Markaryd as soon as politicians at regional or national levels put him under pressure' (*Smålänningen* 3 September 2002, p. 25). The Social Democrat was equally caustic: 'I have had no direct criticism for speaking out the way I did [in January], but I have heard indirectly that what I said [then] was not befitting a municipal commissioner representing the Social Democrats. The morality that I live by is that one should stand by one's word, but [the Christian Democratic commissioner] does not have that kind of morality' (*Smålänningen* 4 September 2002, p. 15).

This verbal fist fight developed in early September, just a few weeks before the national general elections. This was certainly not a coincidence, since local policies towards asylum-seekers turned out to be the most prominent issue in the municipality's pre-election debate. About this time, information was leaked that the Swedish Migration Board planned to locate another 40 asylum-seekers to Markaryd. A leading Christian Democrat reacted strongly to the news: 'Enough is enough. We must raise our voices and put an end to this.' In his view, the present situation had arisen mainly because of the shortcomings of the Migration Board and its failure to inform the municipal authorities about the amount of asylum-seekers to be located to Markaryd in the spring. As already mentioned, the Migration Board had at the time only negotiated with the privately owned municipal housing company. Hence, the politician went on to argue, it was '[t]he ineptitude of the Migration Board that had created antagonism and xenophobia. As politicians, we must take the concerns of the inhabitants seriously and we must dare to say no. The townspeople suffer and those 20-25 persons who have received permanent residence permits and who have been permitted to stay on here suffer as well'. As a further point, he added that it was wrong to 'mix so many nationalities in one place'. Now, he concluded, it was imperative to 'sort out the present problems and let the wounds heal before more asylum-seekers are received' (*Smålänningen* 3 September 2002, p. 12).

When *Smålänningen* asked the national political parties represented in the municipal assembly about their stance on whether or not Markaryd should receive more asylum-seekers, the answers displayed a clear-cut and restrictive tendency. Only one political party, the Leftists, indicated a willingness to receive more asylum-seekers, albeit with the caveat that all of those received would be expected to abide and live by Swedish law. Other than that, local consensus was striking. The Conservatives underlined the importance of the asylum-seekers 'making a societal contribution' and that it was unacceptable to have them receiving grants without working. The Social Democrats said a clear 'no', explaining that the present numbers amounted to what a municipality the size of Markaryd could handle. The Green Party also said a resounding 'no' and referred to the 'great problems that had been encountered' during the year. The agrarian Centre Party stated that the municipal reception service for refugees who had been granted asylum had worked well throughout its time of operation, but that the municipality could do nothing about how many asylum-seekers the Migration Board chose to receive on a national basis. However, the number of people received at the reception centre should not be increased, its representatives held. The Christian Democrats also said no. The municipality of Markaryd had at present enough asylum-seekers in relation to its resources, they argued, and went on to conclude: 'First we must solve our present problems. Then we can start thinking about receiving more people' (*Smålänningen* Med mera-bilaga 'Val 2002', 6 September 2002, p. 10-11).

Initially, the liberal People's Party seemed to dodge the question. The municipality should continue to receive asylum-seekers, its representatives said, provided that financial circumstances allowed and space was available for their accommodation. In line with the party's stance at the national level (see Chapter 6), the representatives emphasised that the asylum-seekers would have to meet certain demands. The caveats that were added thereafter made the party's spokesmen the most blatantly restrictive of all the local politicians interviewed on their views towards asylum-seekers. The reader should take note of the specific expressions used in their statement: 'It is vital that the Migration Board receive the resources necessary to shorten the periods needed for inquiry and that *unwanted people* can be *weeded out* early in the process. In case they *slip through* [the net] anyway, they should be *taken care of* and evicted if they do not behave properly' (*Smålänningen* Med mera-bilaga 'Val 2002', 6 September 2002, p. 10-11; my emphasis added). Representatives of the local populist party named the Alternative were not interviewed by the newspaper, but in case they had been, it is doubtful whether they would have expressed themselves much more colourfully than the People's Party representatives did. Thus, a large part of the asylum-seekers were being depicted as 'unwanted'. Those deemed to belong to that group were to be 'weeded out' and should not be given the chance to 'slip through'. If they still managed to do so, however, they should 'be taken care of'. The representatives who stated these views may very well have spoken before thinking. Even so, their choice of wording was gross and distasteful.

In early September, *Smålänningen* ran an article about pre-election sentiments in the town, underlining that the issue about the asylum-seekers had been turned into a paramount concern in the local election debate. Several of the townspeople interviewed by the paper's journalist vied that this was the most crucial issue. However, they also felt that it was not really seen as proper to address it and that they did not wish to be seen as 'racists'. Giving voice to two individuals purportedly representing this local public opinion, the journalist interviewed two men, both of whom were around 60 years of age. 'We must establish some law and order in our society', one of them said. 'We receive far too many asylum-seekers. The community is too small for this large an amount. I also think that those who commit a crime should be evicted from here at once.... Our society has become decadent and law and order has ceased to function satisfactorily'. The other man largely echoed those views, saying that 'the politicians should do something about it and manage the issue better. There should be stricter rules concerning who may come in here and who may stay on' (*Smålänningen* 9 September 2002, p. 11). Here, the power of the local press was vividly borne out. The importance of which voices are selected and allowed to articulate their opinions could hardly be illustrated more clearly. On this particular occasion, only two voices were selected; both of which were harshly critical towards foreigners and equally pointed in their distrust of the politicians' handling of the matter. Still, the way they were permitted to speak out, and the forum that they were given to do so, created an unwarranted and false impression of representativity.

Thus, on the eve of the elections, the issue about the asylum-seekers and their perceived links to the increased criminality in Markaryd was a highly salient one. Local politicians seemed almost unanimous in their assessments that too many asylum-seekers had been received in Markaryd and that it was the Migration Board that was to blame for the large number of asylum-seekers that, all of a sudden, had become located to the municipality. Seemingly, the politicians mirrored local public opinion and took a large part in constructing and leading it. An important role was also played by *Smålänningen*. Very few asylum-seekers were given voice on its news pages, and we have seen that those who were given the opportunity to express their perspectives largely came to be depicted as the exceptions that proved the rules.

Markaryd Goes National

As we have seen, events in Markaryd were critical enough to merit a visit by the minister then responsible for migration issues in Sweden. The reason that the national political establishment had paid a visit to the local community was possibly to help calm things down. This was apparently needed, as one national actor—the Swedish Migration Board—was attributed a rogue's characteristics in the local plot. In Markaryd the Board had the potential of serving as an alternative Other, that helped to promote local togetherness in an air of frustrated contempt of the perceived ineptitude and heavy-handedness at the central level of governance. In that sense, it might actually have served to take some pressure off the asylum-seekers themselves, as they were not the only culprits to be identified. However, we have seen that the minister's efforts to placate emotions that were running high were more counterproductive than helpful in this enterprise, at least in the short run. They produced a rift within the local political community, at the same time as they seemed to reinforce the sense that the local community was forlorn and forsaken by national politicians and their implementing agencies. So actually, both the central authorities and the asylum-seekers located to Markaryd were depicted as bad guys in the local debate. If anything, the as-cribed roles seemed to reinforce each other and the conveyed image of Mark-aryd was one of a community squeezed in between two highly undesired and harmful forces. Markaryd was, quite simply, left on its own.

There was, however, another facet to take into account as well. Not only did the national heavily impose itself on the local, but the events in Markaryd also spilled over to the national level. In early June, the Social Democratic commis-sioner had, together with prominent local politicians from four other municipali-ties in southern Sweden (Tingsryd, Lessebo, Olofström and Uppvidinge), had a meeting with representatives of the Swedish Migration Board. The reason they got together was that the four municipalities had all experienced rising crime rates that had coincided in time with increases in the numbers of asylum-seekers received at their local reception centres. After the meeting, the commissioner reported that 'We received a promise which, in principle, said that no more criminal individuals will be sent here. If it is at all possible to promise such a thing in the first place' (*Smålänningen* 7 June 2002, p. 12).

The article that reported on the meeting indicated the essence and the tone of the deliberations. The thorniest issue had been how to prevent individuals with a proven criminal record from coming to Sweden and applying for asylum, even if they knew from the outset that such an application would most probably be fruitless. According to what was stated in *Smålänningen*, the main problem was that these persons used the time of inquiry to commit new crimes. The sug-gested solution was therefore to establish a special fast line of inquiry for cases where the applicants' prospects of being granted asylum were bleak due to a criminal record. During such an inquiry, the applicants were to be housed in fa-cilities separated from the regular reception centres. These lodgings were provi-sionally termed 'units of special accommodation'. It remained an open question as to whereabouts in Sweden such units were eventually to be located (*Smålänningen* 7 June 2002, p. 12).

At the meeting, the commissioner representing Markaryd had suggested that, in the future, the authorities should refrain from 'mixing so many nationali-ties of asylum-seekers in the same municipality'. With this statement, he articu-lated the previously encountered and common myth that immigrants can be neatly subdivided into different categories based on essentialised ethnic, cultural and religious characteristics, and that these categories should be kept apart so as not to permit dangerous frictions and conflict to occur. The representatives of the Migration Board were negative to the commissioner's suggestion, however, on the grounds that it was impossible to predict the future composition of the groups of refugees who decided to come to Sweden. Furthermore, the commis-sioner and his colleagues from the other municipalities wished to ask the Swed-ish government to investigate whether asylum-seekers with a criminal record could not be evicted already at the national border. This would, however, neces-sitate amendments to the Schengen Treaty of border controls and so this idea was also not practicable (*Smålänningen* 7 June 2002, p. 12).

Implementing the Fast Lane

From subsequent press reports, it became clear that the new procedures suggested by the Migration Board at the meeting in June had actually been in operation for some time, at least as a trial activity. Already in March, the southern Swedish branch of the Migration Board had started up a fast lane of inquiry for persons with a suspected criminal record. Even though these suspects had not been dispersed to the special accommodation units, their cases were observed with extraordinary attention, and in instances where the branch had received reports of renewed criminal activity, the fast lane had been activated. If no reasons for asylum were subsequently found to apply, negative decisions could be reached speedily and the individuals promptly evicted. Since the start of the pilot activity, 45 cases had been dealt with in this manner, all of which had consequently resulted in the final decision not to grant asylum (*Smålänningen* 7 October 2002, p. 14).

One of the four Migration Board officials involved in the new programme was interviewed by *Smålänningen*. He claimed to be fully aware of the problems that had occurred in Markaryd: 'A few people have ruined things for the others. Those who commit criminal acts become highly visible and it can easily follow that the image of all the others deteriorates as well' (*Smålänningen* 7 October 2002, p. 14). This seems indeed to be a case of the well-known principles for stereotype-formation being put into practice, as a few disorderly individuals are taken to represent a whole category of people. The Migration Board official's statement practically echoed the diagnosis offered by the secretary of the local council for crime prevention in Markaryd: 'Few of them commit crimes, but those who do are so much more active' (*Smålänningen* 5 December 2002, p. 12). And indeed, despite these statements, the fact that the perpetrators of the crimes actually constituted a minority did not seem to rub off at all on the local discussion. The manner in which the incidents were reported by the newspaper did little to dispel the notion that asylum-seekers were more inclined to commit crimes than representatives of the majority population. In all likelihood, such references either left such stereotypes unscathed, or at worst, helped to reinforce them.

A few days after the first reports on the perceived successes of the trial activity, there was another article in *Smålänningen* indicating that the fast-lane inquiry system may not have been so efficient after all. Those asylum-seekers who knew that their reasons for asylum were less than solid often chose to hide their true identities and thus had no personal identification documents on them when crossing the national border. Therefore, it was often impossible to establish their country of origin, meaning that no evictions could be made in accordance with the fast-lane inquiry system, since the Swedish authorities could not know what country to evict them to. A coordinator at the southern branch of the Migration Board estimated that about 80 per cent of new asylum-seekers lacked valid documents upon arrival (*Smålänningen* 11 October 2002, p. 22). Caution was therefore called for, and warnings made that the authorities should not be too triumphant about the new system. Even so, one influential representative of the political elite in neighbouring Ljungby greeted the establishment of the system as a major achievement on the part of Markaryd. For, he argued, the municipality had managed to make people at the national political level aware of the problems in the locality, and the formulae proposed by the local representatives had been translated into national practice. Moreover, all of this had contributed to a greater degree of restrictive measures being taken in the treatment of asylum applications which, according to the interviewee, was a good thing (interview J. Johansson).

Different Sections, Diverging Stories

As mentioned in passing above, during the summer of 2002, an event publicised nationwide occurred in the province of Småland, as about 50 people started a fight on a beach, using axes, knives and screwdrivers as weapons. It soon emerged that all of those involved were asylum-seekers, and it was later made explicitly clear that they were Roma people, who had come to Sweden from Eastern Europe (*Sydsvenska Dagbladet* 7 June 2002; *Dagens Nyheter* 12 June 2002).

A few days later, an editorial in *Smålänningen* commented upon the beach fight and other recent cases of violent clashes in Sweden that had involved asylum-seekers. It rebuffed the argument that the main reason for these problems was that Sweden 'had received more refugees than it could handle'. Rather, the piece argued, the Migration Board, the police and the social security branch of local government simply had to manage their tasks better. Concern was expressed to the effect that vigilante groups were starting to form locally and that the Migration Board seemed to greet such a worrying development as something essentially positive (*Smålänningen* 14 June 2002, p. 2). However, the editorial is not very likely to have had a major impact on public opinion in the municipality. As already mentioned, too few people read this section of the paper, as it was not written by local actors, and so it was prone to be overridden and contradicted by other sections of the newspaper.

And indeed, there were frequently such divergences of opinion between the editorials and the news pages in *Smålänningen*. The editorial pages repeatedly devoted space to the issues of immigration policies and the reception of refugees, whereby they argued the case of pursuing open, flexible and liberal policies. The editorialists made it clear that they did not want a 'Danish development' in Sweden and that they viewed it as imperative that Sweden not shy away from international moral obligations. As we have seen, however, the news pages most often told another story. And since they were much more influential among the readers, the net effect of the predominance of critical voices within these pages was to create an overall negative impression of asylum-seekers in Markaryd in particular, and, most probably, of immigrants in general.

Background Factors: Why Markaryd?

It is not difficult to see how local news media reports, such as those in Markaryd, can be taken out of their context to be used by propagators for stricter immigration policies. They can easily be employed to feed xenophobic sentiments, as well as to legitimise populist policies aimed at further marginalising and squeezing out immigrants and asylum-seekers. The media thus have a huge responsibility to shoulder. Unless they do so, they can easily turn into peddlers of stereotypes and unsavoury enemy images that can never be falsified. When confronted with a barrage of negative reporting about crimes purportedly committed by asylum-seekers, readers, who are convinced from the outset that the foreigners ought to go home, are prone to become even more entrenched in their views, and those who are ambivalent are likely to start to lean more clearly towards restrictive views (cf. Entman & Rojecki 2000:57). The street brawl in Strömsnäsbruk recounted above, for example, certainly indicates how scapegoating phenomena might contribute to vicious circles of ever-increasing distrust and violence. In such cases, societal discourse—much aided by the contribution of the media—translates risks into imminent dangers and the need for preventive action may, as a consequence, start to be widely discerned.

Smålänningen was not, however, the sole or perhaps even the most important actor in the arena. In this sense, the local newspaper certainly lived up to at least some of its self-proclaimed ambition to be a mirror of events rather than an active actor itself. Why only some of its ambition? Well, exactly because the paper acted as a mirror and thus reflected the local majority's sizzling displeasure about the perceived developments. And whether the editors liked it or not, this made it a powerful local actor in its own right. This said, it seems fair to say that the greatest responsibility for the tense situation rested with other local actors; the politicians, the traders and the council for crime prevention. The leading politicians, who represented the major national political parties, should have known better than to fuel the situation further by polarising the arguments. Their positions should have made it possible for them to act as moderating influences on the brusque suggestions aired by the traders and the council for crime prevention. This was however the one route they did not opt for. Moreover, a precondition for their societal impact was that they could freely use the newspaper as an arena, and there seemed to be few restrictions in this regard. And it was perhaps easier said than done for the local editors to free themselves from these local dynamics and deny the most prominent actors in the community access to the floor.

It is, however, too simple to make do with actor-based explanations when trying to assess why sentiments in Markaryd were so pointedly negative. In order to delve somewhat deeper into the issue and see the fuller contours of the local community's almost unanimously manifested wish to shut the asylum-seekers out, there are some background factors that need to be taken into account.

A Downturn According to Several Indices

If it is hard to express pride in one's own group, and hence in oneself, it is close at hand to voice outrage towards the behaviour and mores associated with Others perceived as deviant. Indeed, collective self-esteem seemed to be at a low point in Markaryd during the year of 2002. For example, although unemployment rates were not alarmingly high in the community itself—there were seasonal variations during the year which made the rates fluctuate between 3 and 4 per cent of the total working force—the figures were markedly higher than for the neighbouring municipalities and also slightly above the corresponding county average. Financially, the year was also a gloomy one for Markaryd. In late summer, it was announced that municipal expenses had to be cut by some 2 million Swedish kronor within the next three-year period (*Smålänningen* 14 August 2002, p. 15). The figures were specified a few weeks later, when the stated overall cuts were further increased. According to the revised figures, as much as 6.3 million kronor had to be slashed from current budgets in a three-year period, mostly due to a huge deficit that the municipality had incurred during the previous year (*Smålänningen* 16 August 2002, p. 13).

Other indicators were equally depressing. Figures were quoted showing that pupils of the nine-year compulsory school in Markaryd performed worse than both the rest of the county and the national average. A staggering 17 per cent of the pupils who finished compulsory school did so without achieving a pass grade in mathematics, Swedish or English. This meant that they would not be eligible to apply to high school. Similarly, 25 per cent of the pupils finished ninth grade without having completed all of the compulsory courses, which was also worse than the county and national average. In a feeble attempt to explain away these statistics, one local politician mused that perhaps the municipal teachers of Markaryd were putting higher demands on their pupils than their counterparts in other municipalities did (*Smålänningen* 19 December 2002, p. 12). And while on the subject of negative news relating to the municipal schools, *Smålänningen* reported shortly before Christmas that a factory, which was situated next to the high school in Markaryd, had been found to emit alarmingly high quantities of carcinogenic substances, such as formaldehyde (*Smålänningen* 18 December 2002, p. 13). Again, there were scant reasons to celebrate.

Also in 2002, the Confederation of Swedish Enterprise presented a list that reviewed how all of the municipalities in Sweden were doing by way of providing a good and stimulating milieu for private enterprise. The neighbouring municipalities of Ljungby and Älmhult were allocated 44th and 53rd positions respectively, whereas Markaryd was found as far down as 200th position among the total 289 municipalities on the list (*Smålänningen* 14 May 2002, p. 7). The figures only helped to contribute to the overall gloomy picture that was being painted locally. They were a component part of a flood of negatively laden indices of what took place in Markaryd during the year, and the newspaper itself certainly depicted an image of a community in crisis.

The point advanced here is not, however, that these circumstances either individually or even as a whole constituted traits of a major societal crisis in Markaryd. Rather, my intention is to show that they were all stories that were dealt with and reported on by the newspaper, which in general played a role in the construction of everyday life in the community. The paper mirrored local sentiments that, at this point, were rather sombre, and thus it to a large extent actually helped to build up a local crisis that was co-constructed and lived by the local inhabitants. And this local atmosphere, I would argue, was a fertile ground on which adverse feelings towards strangers could grow and flourish and where the dynamics of scapegoating could be set in motion. This was especially so since there were relatively few positively defined characteristics that joined the members of the majority in-group together. And in such circumstances, deviant Others are certainly very effective in defining the borders delineating the local Us. So, indeed, what bonds were there to hold the majority in-group together?

A Confused Local Identity?

In the very first days of 2002, there was an interesting and rather indicative news item retold on the Markaryd pages of *Smålänningen*. The municipal authorities had contributed half a million Swedish kronor towards a project run by a shareholding company by the name of 'Markaryd Growth Ltd.'. The task of the company was to place Markaryd onto the outside world's 'mental map'. To this end, it aimed to develop a symbol of Markaryd which could facilitate the marketing of the municipality both nationally and internationally. There had hitherto been no such symbol, which was attributed to the fact that Markaryd had 'no nationally or internationally famous persons, no monuments, no trademarks or logos, no companies or activities that people outside the municipality could associate the community with' (*Smålänningen* 3 January 2002, p. 12). Quite simply, Markaryd was considered to be too nondescript, too anonymous and too little known to the outside world. However, as if to bring further evidence to this diagnosis of Markaryd's facelessness, as well as revealing its apparent apathy towards such a predicament, the paper reported only about a month later that the project had been dismantled. The reason for this had quite simply been the lack of interest among local firms and companies. They just did not believe in the project and did not wish to contribute to it (*Smålänningen* 6 February 2002, p. 10).

This story seems to suggest that there was a less than developed sense of local identity in Markaryd. Nor did there seem to be a prevalent sense of belonging to a regional community. Indeed, regional belonging was seen as so ambiguous that two representatives of the Conservative party petitioned to the municipal assembly that a local referendum be held concerning what county Markaryd should belong to. They argued that since the municipality was situated at the very southern borders of the county, many inhabitants in fact had more ties to the neighbouring counties of Halland and Skåne than to the county of Kronoberg to which they belonged administratively. The petitioners further held that there were many indicators that local inhabitants turned to the neighbouring counties for certain key services. When, for example, young people had to choose which university to apply to, they were prone to choose Lund, situated in Skåne, rather than Växjö, Kronoberg's regional centre. Likewise, when the inhabitants needed to go by air, they did so from Halmstad in Halland or Ängelholm in Skåne, not from Växjö. And when they were in need of hospital care, they again went to Halmstad rather than Växjö (*Smålänningen* 23 April 2002, p. 15). The petitioning politicians could also have added that, when Markaryd town-dwellers needed to go to a health-care centre, they were often prone to cross the county border to visit the one in Knäred in Halland which, according to *Smålänningen*, was deemed to be more accessible and to offer lower prices for services, such as issuing medical certificates (*Smålänningen* 11 October 2002, p. 23).

The referendum idea was supported some weeks later in a letter-to-the-editor, that was signed by a leading county level representative of the Conservative party (*Smålänningen* 23 May 2002, p. 24). Thus, the proposal to have a local referendum on the issue of Markaryd's county membership seemed to be prominently placed on the local political agenda (*Smålänningen* 20 August 2002, p. 20). The subject reappeared in slightly different forms on numerous occasions later during the year. Thus, the dissatisfaction with Markaryd's ascribed regional belonging seemed fairly widespread.

Stereotyping Markaryd

Any writer analysing and describing stereotyping phenomena runs the risk of constructing similar stereotypes him-/herself regarding his/her object of study (Lindberg 1998:9). In the analysis made above, Markaryd has been painted in rather gloomy colours. And so it should be pointed out that, although there was unquestionably a compact wall of resistance and adversity in the community towards the placement of asylum-seekers at the local reception centre, this is not to say that all of the inhabitants of Markaryd towed this line. Indeed, there were certainly individuals who wished to distance themselves from majority sentiments. While telling such a discrepant story, however, one voice did little to contradict the overall view of Markaryd as a den of intolerance, suspicion and budding xenophobia. In a letter-to-the-editor, a woman who taught Swedish to asylum-seekers reacted strongly to the negative publicity that surrounded them. She wrote that the asylum-seekers should first and foremost be treated as fellow human beings who were on the run from mortal danger. They had not come to abuse the social welfare system, she wrote, but to reconstruct their lives and earn their own living. The teacher therefore suggested that the asylum-seekers be given the opportunity to work in the afternoons, while studying Swedish during the morning hours. They should be viewed as an asset, not as a burden. In conclusion, she warned about the development of covert everyday racism among 'ordinary decent folks'. It was this kind of everyday racism, she said, that made people look away when the police came to pick up desperate people who were about to be evicted from the country. These turned-away faces made her think of the Nazi period of the 1930s, when far too many people conveniently looked in the other direction (*Smålänningen* 22 May 2002, p. 24). Painted in these rash colours, few rays of light could be discerned in Markaryd.

However, there were indeed committed individuals among the majority population who strove hard to make a difference. In order to counter the looming spectre of racism, nationally renowned lecturers were called upon to cover precisely the subject of racism, both for the eighth and ninth graders at the compulsory school and for the municipality high school. Among those asked to speak to the children was a survivor from Auschwitz, as well as the mother of John Hron, a young boy who, in 1995, had been tortured and murdered by neo-Nazis while refusing to betray his friends (*Smålänningen* 15 February 2002, p. 17; 21 March 2002, p. 15).

In a community where polarisation prevailed and where there seemed to be no dialogue between the majority population and the asylum-seekers, contacts between the two groups were sorely needed. The local football club thus made an effort to establish some channels of communication. It had applied for funding from resources that the Swedish government had allocated to promote local democracy. The club planned to use the means to 'involve persons from different ethnic backgrounds' in its activities (*Smålänningen* 26 March 2002, p. 13). One could argue, of course, that it would not necessarily have required additional financial means to do this—indeed, apart from perhaps an extra trainer and a few extra footballs, it is difficult to imagine what else was considered necessary to get the project up and running. The club did however serve as a channel for at least one asylum-seeker to enter into the community of the majority. *Smålänningen* recounted the story of 14-year-old Ruslan who had come to Sweden from Kazakhstan some six months earlier. He had found his way to Markaryd and the local football club, where he was now playing on the team. His coach—certainly adhering to some kind of exoticising stereotype—characterised him as a 'rough diamond'. The boy said that he enjoyed life in Sweden, since everyone was kind, the air was clean and one could go outside without having to worry about one's personal safety. It was still unclear, however, whether Ruslan would acquire a permanent residence permit and, according to the newspaper's assessment, that issue was not likely to be settled for quite some time yet (*Smålänningen* 25 July 2002, p. 25).

So, Ruslan had an unusual talent, which is almost certainly what made life easier for him in everyday Markaryd. He turned out to be the exception that proved the rule. In a similarly unusual success story, *Smålänningen* wrote about the newly appointed principal of one of the municipal compulsory schools. She was a woman, she was single and 15 years before she had arrived as a refugee from Hungary. All of this together made her an unlikely choice as a principal but somehow, the paper observed, the appointment committee had envisaged her apparent disadvantages to be her advantage (*Smålänningen*, 2 September 2002, p. 14). Again, what was revealing about this item was that it was deemed newsworthy in the first place. Had the appointment been made without being treated as big news by the newspaper, the integration of immigrants into everyday life in Markaryd could have been judged to have made considerable headway. But this sadly does not seem to be the case. Rather, these two individual success stories can actually be read as confirmation of the basic stereotypes that existed in Markaryd about immigrants in general.

Concluding the Case: Assessing Markaryd

Quite clearly, the articles in *Smålänningen* that reported on local discontent in Markaryd had a bias. There were instances when sweeping allegations were passed on to the readership without proper corroboration by evidence. There was also a total dominance of cases where a multitude of voices spoke out critically about asylum-seekers, and no voices at all were heard speaking up on their behalf, let alone voices belonging to the asylum-seekers themselves. I brought this up in an interview with two leading representatives of *Smålänningen*—the editor-in-chief and the news editor. Given this information, they were both inclined to agree that there had perhaps been an unremedied imbalance in the news reports from Markaryd. They even conceded that certain safety mechanisms may not have been activated in the course of writing and printing the articles. There was often, they explained, a certain distance, a communication gap even, between the central editorial staff and the local editors, such as those in Markaryd. The central staff tried to help and support them over the phone as much as they could but, especially when time was scarce just before printing, it might well be that this safety net failed to protect very much against bias. There was definitely more control involved when articles were written in the central newsroom. It was also hinted to me that a position as local editor in a municipality the size of Markaryd was often not a journalist's first preference, leaving those who were perhaps slightly less motivated to fill the vacancies.

Whatever the reasons behind it, it is an inescapable fact that a prevalent mode of procedure in *Smålänningen's* coverage of the Markaryd case was to let voices speak out that were deeply critical about asylum-seekers and the benefits they purportedly enjoyed. Such voices belonged to, for example, local politicians, civil servants or traders, and by letting them speak, the paper could create an impression of just passing on objective information that happened to be 'out there' anyway. As already noted, however, the selection of voices is far from neutral and objective in itself (cf. Erjavec 2003, Pietikäinen 2003). The asylum-seekers in Markaryd were most often associated with crime and disorderliness in the news reports. Then it is perhaps not surprising, especially given the paper's extensive readership and the popularity of the news section, that the community remained divided and polarised, and that a climate of suspicion prevailed. This was further compounded by the downward turn of several indicators of local well-being during the year of study. When the sun shines, life seems brighter, but the sun was apparently not shining much on Markaryd during the year of 2002.

According to the image conveyed by the local newspaper, risks to socio-cultural values were abundant, and most of them were deemed to have been brought by the asylum-seekers. What was, by all appearances, even worse, was that such risks were already considered to have evolved into imminent dangers and threats to cherished everyday mores, as well as to property and personal safety. This change in perception was most probably an underlying reason behind the clashes that were suffered by the community in the same year. The general elections that took place during the autumn did nothing to help matters, since the presence of the asylum-seekers, the consequences that were believed to emanate from it, and the prospects of integrating the newcomers into the host community, all together constituted the most topical and burning issues during that year's municipal pre-election campaign in Markaryd. This exacerbated the climate of polarisation even further, not least since only one minor political party (the Leftists) distanced itself from the prejudicial views about immigrants. The rest simply joined in the chorus.

Overall, there certainly seemed to be ample connections between the stereotype-forming dynamics that depicted the immigrants as unreliable, deceitful, troublesome and generally unwanted, on the one hand, and the heightened experience of socio-cultural risks to the community of the majority, on the other. The most unruly members of the collective of asylum-seekers were taken to represent their entire general category, and so the community was seen to be beset by risks to community values as well as imminent dangers to property, well-being and safety. In the stories that were told about them, the asylum-seekers were likened to misbehaving guests, at times even to parasites, and were generally portrayed as a wide-ranging burden to the community.

Nothing good could be gained from this kind of rough-shod imagery. Polarisation increased almost daily between 'Swedes' and 'foreigners', between 'hosts' and 'guests', between 'residents' and 'ethnic groups' of foreigners, that allegedly should not be 'mixed' into their new Swedish host societies. Instead, they should be kept apart as far as possible, because if they were not, violent and fateful clashes and explosions might occur. Indeed, racism and xenophobia were lurking even among the gentle folks of the settled majority and the everyday rhythm appeared to be on the point of being shattered. There was a resulting lived crisis experienced by residents and asylum-seekers alike, but this, apparently, was the *only* thing they had in common.

6. Absent from the Everyday:
The Ljungby Story

Ljungby achieved the status of 'town' in the mid 1930s. Thanks to the expansion of local industries, above all machine manufacturing, the town grew to its present size, which is about 14 000 inhabitants in the town itself and a total 27 000 in the municipality (www.ljungby.se). The job market is stable by national comparison and unemployment figures are low. There is currently however some local concern over the fact that the municipality has a negative migration pattern; less people move into the municipality than out of it. There is a growing awareness that Ljungby might not in the future be immune to general declines in the national and international economies, and that the tight texture of medium-technology industries in the area might not be as sturdy as it used to be during most of the 20th century. Thus, local politicians are intent on changing the prevailing image of Ljungby as a stronghold for the 'male, mechanised and lowly educated' (interview Jönsson). Proactive strategies are being designed to meet the challenges of contemporary times. One aspect of this is, for instance, that a branch of Växjö University has recently been established in the town.

The inhabitants look upon their municipality as a small-town; they have no illusions of it being a metropolis. Nonetheless, as a small-town, it equally clearly has some tangible trademarks, which is made apparent in the reports about what sites tourists tend to visit, and also in comments by local townspeople about what they take pride in regarding the town. Since Ljungby received its township privileges relatively late, these sites tend to be less architectural landmarks and historical buildings than places for cultural expositions. The unique-

ness of the Museum of Legends is repeatedly pointed out. In its interactive milieu, the visitor is invited to make a stunning journey, treated with ingredients
from local legends about spirits, trolls, fairies and pixies, and is also provided
with some explanations how the stories arose. The other major cultural venue
most frequently mentioned by visitors and townspeople is the Ljungberg museum, devoted to the work of, and also named after, a well-known local artist.

Another characteristic frequently mentioned about Ljungby is its beautiful
surroundings, the landscape, forests and lakes. The manager of the largest local
hotel claimed this factor to be the principal one accounting for most tourists'
visits to the municipality (*Smålänningen* 18 July 2002, p. 1, 4). According to the
tourist office staff, foreign tourists above all sought access to unspoiled nature
and wished to have active holidays that included bicycling, canoeing, fishing,
camping and elk trekking. 'Always these elks', the official remarked
(*Smålänningen* 18 September 2002, p. 7). When a project was launched with the
aim of boosting local growth and development by pooling resources of private
enterprise and voluntary associations, it was held that the natural environment
constituted Ljungby's greatest asset. The project indicated optimism and entre-
preneurship, and its coordinator was confident that the key to strong local development was that Ljungby really tried to exploit its resources as a resort for active holidays close to nature (*Smålänningen* 3 October 2002, p. 3).

Needless to say, there are also other component parts to what could be seen
as a local identity. A large part of the Ljungby townspeople speak highly of the
local ice hockey club, Troja (Troy). For them, the Troja club is undoubtedly a
part of the local identity. On my visit to the town, I noticed that the municipal
commissioner had its insignia in prime position on his bookshelf. When asked
what he spontaneously would associate with Ljungby, a newly recruited municipal information officer mentioned Troja, the 19th century singer Kristina Nilsson and the previously mentioned artist Ljungberg, in that particular order
(*Smålänningen* 6 February 2002, p. 6). A one-time immigrant to Ljungby recounted how he several years before had visited Stockholm. Upon mentioning
the name of his hometown to a taxi driver, he had received the response:
'Ljungby? Oh, isn't that where they only have one traffic light and a hockey
club by the name of Troja?' (*Smålänningen* 10 April 2002, p. 28). Doubtless, the
hockey club is one of the town's most important trademarks. When the club ran
into financial difficulties during 2002, local supporters organised a campaign to
its aid which gathered more than 1100 subscribing members (*Smålänningen* 6
March 2002, p. 4). Almost on a daily basis, *Smålänningen* informed its readers
how much of the 2 million kronor needed had so far been collected. In the end,
the local politicians decided to drop half of the municipality's financial claim on
Troja, ostensibly because of the large PR value associated with it and the important functions the club fulfilled in providing a social meeting point for the local
youth (*Smålänningen* 3 April 2002, p. 1, 4).

Making a Detour: Looking Back to 1987

Stereotypes and stories about the strange have longevity of their own. They travel across space and are largely persistent across time. Yet, there is also a certain potential for change. In order to take these aspects into account I decided, when designing the study of Ljungby, to include a point of reference further back in time so as to put the more contemporary discussions into perspective. For several reasons I chose to settle for the year of 1987. This was a year when the Wall was still intact, and Mikhail Gorbachev had barely embarked on his reform agenda in the Soviet Union. In other words, the political map of Europe was still rigidly divided into two opposing camps. Threatening as this condition certainly was, it also provided some elementary security. The Other was well known, and s/he was an ideological foe. Globalisation had not yet become the buzzword of popular discussion or academic debates. And multiculturalism was far from on the top of any political agenda in Sweden or Europe.

For the year of 1987, the town of Ljungby had in an agreement with the Swedish Immigrant Agency made the commitment to accept about 40 refugees annually. The Agency wished Ljungby to accept a larger number for 1988, but the municipal authorities refused to do so, arguing that housing was a problem, and that several landlords were unwilling to rent their flats out to refugees. Little about these frictions reached the pages of *Smålänningen* however. There were only two reports of disagreement between the local social security office and individual immigrants. On one occasion, a refugee couple had refused to sign a renting contract, complaining that they had been promised a flat with a kitchen, but it turned out that it was only a kitchenette. In the other case, a refugee chose to dump all of his furniture outside the social security office, in a protest against having to live in a three-room flat, in spite of his constantly expressed wish that he for economic reasons be given a one-room flat. Apart from these incidents, however, there were few disturbances that reached public attention.

Rather, the Ljungby town dwellers were presented with accounts that suggested that, although there were indeed groups of immigrants and refugees present in the town, they lived an existence almost totally separated from that of the majority population. Numerous efforts were therefore made to bring the majority and minority populations closer to each other, through the Red Cross, Save the Children, the religious congregations, and the local chapter of the Labour Trade Union. Bridge-building is definitely a key metaphor which could be employed here.

Characteristically, the inhabitants of Ljungby would be invited to attend some kind of café gathering, where one or several immigrant groups would treat them with dishes that were presented as typical for their nation or ethnic group, and play music likewise deemed to be typical, or perform folk dances. And then, after a gathering of this kind, the two groups, the majority and the minority, would again be separated and go on living their existence secluded from each other. This nature of things was much exacerbated by the way that the foreign influences were presented. Swedish was beyond any doubt the norm, and the Other could well be a positive encounter, but if it so happened, it was maybe exciting but definitely exotic. You may visit the exotic, and you may even taste it, study it and subject it to scrutiny, but you will probably never, ever consider making it a part of your daily routines and existence. The exotic is still the deviant and hence also potentially risky.

And so, the small groups of refugees in Ljungby, which in 1987 mainly consisted of Chinese, Romanians and Eritreans, were once in a while invited to organised get-togethers with the majority population and given the opportunity to introduce what was perceived to be their 'culture' to the town dwellers. All of this was ostensibly done to erase prejudice, tear down barriers and extend bridges between the two groups. As already pointed out, 'bridge' was indeed a word aptly chosen in this context, since majority and minority groups otherwise seemed to live on separate islands. And although this kind of island existence can of course be seen as being less than satisfactory, as suggested above, it was rarely seen as a problem or as something bringing risk in its wake. Either the nature of the prejudice never really reached the local news; or it was never considered to be that much of a problem in the first place. The only exception was represented by the letters-to-the-editor department where, occasionally, letters with a racist tinge were published. Typically, the writers would argue that obligatory mother-tongue education was a waste of money and actually an act of discrimination against the Swedish majority children. It deserves to be noticed, however, that these letters provoked counter-reactions, both from other letter writers, as well as from the editorial department, which took pains to dispel popular misconceptions about welfare benefits for refugees.

Otherwise, *Smålänningen* was brimming with articles about local inhabitants that had, for one reason or another, chosen to go abroad and spend some time there. This was consistently described as something out of the ordinary, and indeed, something worth writing about. The normal thing in 1987 certainly seemed to be to remain within the confines of the local community. Quite often, the people that did go away had a religious zeal and several were dispatched to foreign countries as missionaries. One representative of the local Filadelfia congregation had, for example, decided to leave for Tanzania, to work there as a missionary for two months. Before embarking on his trip, he remarked that the region he was going to was 'dominated by Muslims'. This was a problem, he conceded, as 'their faith is deeply ingrained and it is often difficult to convert them'.

Judging by the day-to-day news coverage mediated by *Smålänningen*, strangers did not on the whole constitute a major concern for Ljungby's community-dwellers in 1987. There were other spectres to worry about, among which were several formidable threats to consider. This was a year of HIV frenzy, and very clearly the HIV/Aids pandemic had already shattered substantial parts of the solid bedrock of existence even in the local community. Drug abuse was another, related theme that evoked public attention. There was surely a linkage to foreign countries regarding both of these themes, albeit not that foreign. Much of the drugs import, as well as HIV infection, was reported to reach Sweden through Copenhagen and other parts of Denmark.

And so, already in 1987, the world was changing. Local ways and customs were beginning to be challenged and Ljungby had, in some ways, already started to become redefined. 'Will the pasta squeeze out the hot dog from the hot dog stands?', one headline asked, albeit jokingly, but still with a worried tone. In the same vein, the town dwellers were treated with reports of environmental degradation on a global scale but with local effects. 'Will the sun get through a hole in the ozone layer above Älmhult?', an inventive headline queried, with regard to the adjacent municipality. So there were certainly global impacts and the HIV/Aids pandemic, drug abuse and environmental hazards topped the agenda. Thus, only scant attention was given to issues involving immigrants and refugees. When 48 out of the 49 politicians comprising the Ljungby municipal assembly were asked what they perceived to be the most prioritised questions for the pending year of 1988, the bulk of them answered child care, old-age health care, finances and environmental protection. None of them mentioned immigration, or the integration or reception of refugees.

There was, however, a neighbouring municipality where immigration issues were considered to be more of a problem. Not surprisingly perhaps, this was Markaryd. In the autumn of 1987, for example, there had been a series of meetings arranged with tenants of the municipal housing company, as there had been numerous local disturbances in two specifically named blocks of housing quarters. According to the newspaper reports, complaints had been made about dirty stairwells, loud and disorderly parties and badly kept laundry rooms. According to the manager of the temporary reception facility, 300 refugees had left Markaryd since January, the lion's share of which had been Eritreans, who had adhered to the custom of throwing parties for their compatriots who were about to leave. The reports from Strömsnäsbruk, in the same municipality of Markaryd, were more positive. There it was expressly reported that there were no manifestations of xenophobia to be seen. Since Strömsnäsbruk, as an old industrial village, was used to receiving migrant workers, it was stated that there were less problems there.

Let us now return to 2002, the main year of study. In some respects, the change of scenery over the ensuing 15 years was clear enough: to name the most obvious contrast, missionary actions definitely seemed to be a thing of the past. In other regards, however, things remained strikingly similar. Stereotypical images of immigrants still prevailed, even if other kinds of socio-cultural risk than the degradation of neighbourhoods tended to be stressed. And although the island structure of majority/minority relations had loosened up slightly, these structures remained rigid and hard to change, as we shall see below. At the same time, some components remained completely the same as in 1987: the letter-to-the-editor section of the local newspaper was still the main site where blatantly racist views could be expressed. Similarly, the neighbouring municipality of Markaryd was still a community which displayed more worrying tendencies than nearby Ljungby. The conflicts there were much more articulated and they had a sense of intensity about them which was unfamiliar in Ljungby.

Contagion Effect?

In the preceding chapter I have recounted how fairly dramatic events occurred in Markaryd in 2002. In this sense, the inhabitants of Ljungby were perhaps living next door to Malice. There are of course multiple channels of communication between two adjacent municipalities. People move across municipal borders in order to work, study, shop, meet their friends and relatives and so on. Therefore and obviously, they communicate across these borders in numerous different ways. Many of the students at the vocational high school in Ljungby, for instance, come from Markaryd. According to the principal of the school in 2002, some of these pupils held 'some pretty sombre ideas' about refugees and asylum-seekers, and from what he could reconstruct, such ideas had been prevalent in Markaryd during at least the past five years or so (interview Ekstrand).

Even though it is not the sole channel of communication, and maybe not even the most important one, Ljungby and Markaryd, together with Älmhult, have the local newspaper, *Smålänningen,* in common. Clearly, the paper is a medium for bringing its interpretation of events in one municipality to the knowledge of the inhabitants of the other. It brings the news from the nearby vicinity to the kitchen tables and living rooms of the local folks, and its influence cannot be neglected. In most cases, however, readers would tend to skip the local news pages that were not devoted to his/her own municipality. According to the polls that *Smålänningen* had conducted, the local Ljungby pages were, as mentioned above, read on a daily basis by 52 per cent of the newspaper's readers, whereas the corresponding figure for the Markaryd pages was about 29 per cent, thus indicating that the tendency to skip the pages of other municipalities than one's own was widespread (Jessen, Nordenstedt & Sandman 1999). However, when stories such as those emanating from Markaryd in 2002 were being served up, with ingredients such as crime, asylum-seekers and public discontent, the reaction would probably tend to be different. There is a great likelihood that such stories would also be read by the inhabitants of neighbouring municipalities (interview Davidsson). The following question is thus justified; namely, if the events in Markaryd had an impact on the local inhabitants in Ljungby, how did this play itself out?

Combating Racism

As a matter of fact, one has to dig rather deep in order to find sentiments of open adversity to strangers in the mainstream society of Ljungby. On the contrary, in the autumn of 2001, a whole week was devoted to the struggle against racism and xenophobia in the town, involving lectures, thematic films and a torch-lit demonstration on the central square ('Projekt 43—Ljungby mot rasism' 2001). This was designed as an offensive, proactive counter-measure against harmful influences. For a while, the town had been affected by gang brawls between skinheads and immigrants in a public park in Ljungby (interview J. Johansson).

Also, the village of Lagan, situated just outside the town, had become the home base for a group of neo-Nazis, which was spreading unrest to other parts of the municipality. From time to time, leaflets with blatantly racist content were distributed in school yards and on the premises of municipal schools.

Despite all this, several of my interviewees stated that there were no manifest problems concerning the relations between the resident population and the immigrants. It was common wisdom that the manufacturing industries in Ljungby had experienced such good times and such stable demand for quite some time that immigrants had been able to integrate naturally and rapidly— provided that they were able and willing to be at the disposal of the labour market. There were, however, different shades and differentiations of view to be noticed here. It was made clear during some interviews that the municipality had actually—and informally—followed a pick-and-choose strategy among those refugees who had received a residence permit in the municipality. Some groups were welcome, while others were not, ostensibly because the municipality had limited resources in terms of interpreters and tuition skills (interview Vong). Clearly, these resources did not cover Somalis and one interviewee asserted that, once upon a time, it had been a mistake to accept Kosovars into the town, as they allegedly did not seem to fit in and were not willing to work and make themselves useful (interview J. Johansson). The myth about the danger of mixing nationalities obviously had its adherents not only in Markaryd, but in Ljungby as well.

Under the surface, worrying signs and indices of xenophobic influences were discernible. A xenophobic populist party, the Swedish Democrats, had for instance scored highly, albeit somewhat below the national average, in a trial election at the high schools in Ljungby during the year. Thus, in order to counteract further xenophobic tendencies, there was in the spring a one-day follow-up of the anti-racist manifestation of the year before. The events were organised on the premises of the most prestigious municipal high school. The main organiser was, apart from the high school, ABF, an educational organisation for adult students associated with the Social Democratic Party. Several lectures were held about Islam and racism, amongst other topics, and one lecture was given by a former neo-Nazi who had opted out of his organisation. The individual talk that earned most publicity in the daily paper was, however, the one given by the father of John Hron, the young boy who in the summer of 1995 had been brutally tortured and murdered by Nazis. The day was rounded off by an international evening featuring singers and dancers from Hungary and Bosnia. According to the organisers, this kind of one-day manifestation would continue for years to come, provided that funding be secured for the purpose (*Smålänningen* 7 March, 22 March 2002).

As a further measure, around Easter time three teachers and six pupils from a municipal elementary school visited the sites of two former concentration camps in Germany, Ravensbrück and Sachsenhausen. The visit clearly made an impression on the pupils: 'We know that there are neo-Nazis even in little Ljungby .... After this journey we realise why we must never forget Nazism and the Holocaust', one of them told the paper (*Smålänningen* 4 April 2002). The main reason for the trip was to find out whether it would be feasible for all ninth-graders to participate in such a trip in the future. The project was indeed realised the following spring (interview Bengtsson).

As suggested by these events, the awareness that racism was lurking in their midst was by and by spreading among the local population. In a public speech in Ljungby on May 1, a Member of Parliament representing the Swedish Leftists said that, with every electoral success of xenophobic parties, he could sense the signs of 'a new political ice age' developing across Europe (*Smålänningen* 2 May 2002). In a similar vein, the municipal Centre Party commissioner cautioned that hostility towards refugees was spreading throughout Sweden and argued that it was imperative to try to thwart those sentiments (*Smålänningen* 7 June 2002).

Local Populism

Local xenophobic populism had gained a concrete face in Ljungby, or at least an ascribed one. A few years earlier, the local populist party the Alternative had, under its charismatic leader, been branded racist in an inflamed local debate. The catalyst had been when the party leader—a local salesman—had argued in favour of a proportional redistribution of newly arrived refugees among all municipalities in Sweden. The suggested calculus was to be made on the basis of their respective population sizes. For Ljungby, this would have meant a fairly drastic cut in reception figures—from 40 to 24 refugees received per annum. This proposal had caused a public outcry—as recounted by the populist politician himself, he had even been branded 'Hitler' by an antagonist at the time (interview R. Johansson).

Originally, the Alternative had arisen from the national populist party of New Democracy when it was in its heyday in the early 1990s. In early 2002, however, internal divisions within the Alternative became apparent, as two leading members in the neighbouring municipality of Älmhult decided to leave the party, protesting against what they saw as xenophobia within the party in Ljungby and Markaryd. Instead, they had chosen to start a local splinter party called the New Alternative (*Smålänningen* 23 May 2002) and, in order to follow up their words with tangible deeds, the representatives of the newly formed party declared their intention to try to promote events through which multicultural influences could give impulses to the local culture. While certainly taking issue with xenophobic sentiments, the splinter party leader's outlook on immigrants seemed fairly influenced by exoticising stereotypes. He thus envisaged 'international days when our immigrants prepare exciting food from different cultures'. 'The equal value of everyone is self-evident to us, and we are dead against racism and xenophobia', he declared (*Smålänningen* 12 August 2002).

In his rebuttal, the leader of the denounced Ljungby branch of the Alternative party stated that he had half a mind to open a libel suit against the former party members. Furthermore, he argued: 'We are quite a different party [in Ljungby] and we do not have any contacts with the Alternative in Älmhult. But we do maintain that we should not receive more refugees than levels of available work and housing permit us to do' (*Smålänningen* 24 May 2002). He went on to say that the Alternative had more members with a foreign background than any other party in Ljungby, and that he personally was in touch with immigrants on a routine basis through his work as a salesman (*Smålänningen* 24 May 2002). Indeed, a week before the national general elections in the autumn, the Ljungby branch of the Alternative ran an advertisement in *Smålänningen*, stating that 'We want to prevent racism and hostility towards immigrants, by promoting that immigrants be given education in both written and spoken Swedish and also that they gain knowledge about our laws. We also want to ensure that immigrants obtain work so that they can take care of their own subsistence' (*Smålänningen* Med mera-bilaga Val 2002, 6 September 2002). Thus, the party representatives tried to describe themselves as anti-racist, even though their actual stance on issues of immigration was often rather ambiguous. For, on the one hand, the Alternative had been the only political party to co-fund the week-long manifestation against racism back in 2001 (cf. 'Projekt 43—Ljungby mot rasism', p. 18). On the other hand, however, statements made by its representatives often betrayed a prejudicial slant towards immigrants.

Perhaps due to the existence of this local populist party—as it might actually have served as a gatekeeper against more hard-core political forces—the pronouncedly xenophobic national parties did not gain access to the municipal assembly in Ljungby. In the end, in fact, the newly formed local branch of the Swedish Democrats decided not to run in the municipal elections (*Smålänningen* 12 September 2002). Even so, it was apparent that some problems remained unsolved in the local political milieu. As one prominent local politician cautioned with regard to the future prospects of openly xenophobic populist parties in Ljungby: 'With the right rebellion leader ['Dackeledare'] they will surely make it in the end' (interview Uvebrant).

Overcoming Marginalisation? Programmes of Integration in Ljungby

After the elections the then municipal commissioner of Ljungby, a Social Democrat, criticised his fellow party member, Swedish Prime Minister Göran Persson, for his failure to include at least one immigrant among his nominees for cabinet posts. 'As a cabinet minister, an immigrant would have been able to comprehend certain problems and assist in solving them in a better way', he claimed (*Smålänningen* 22 October 2002, p. 6). The question is, then, how did the local politicians live up to their responsibilities? How were the issues of asylum-seekers, refugees and immigrants tackled in Ljungby?

The answer to the second question is that these issues were largely absent from the public agenda. The contrast with the concurrent political storm that was brewing in Markaryd is striking. On one occasion, national parliamentarians representing the different political parties assembled for a hearing among high school students, and were asked questions regarding immigration and refugees (*Smålänningen* 22 January 2002). The procedure was repeated later on in the year at a similar activity attended by the local politicians (*Smålänningen* 17 April 2002, p. 6). In neither case did *Smålänningen* provide any further details about the discussion.

Another report regarded a hands-on activity programme for immigrants in Ljungby, which showed that at least some local activists perceived integration efforts hitherto to have been less than optimal. The programme itself was a joint venture between the job centre, the social security bureau and the municipal establishment for the education of adult students. The main idea was to rapidly integrate the immigrants into everyday life, the key to which was believed to be the access to meaningful work. The project staff had primarily approached small and medium-sized enterprises, since these seemed more willing than larger companies to accept trainees from the programme. The organisers' ambition was to find permanent or at least durable jobs for the trainees within two years. After this period, it was hoped, they were to achieve self-sufficiency. Prospects for hiring personnel seemed especially good within the manufacturing industry and the health care sector. Sports clubs and other leisure associations were also contacted by the organisers, and the immigrants themselves were strongly urged to join such clubs in order to make their recreational time more meaningful both for themselves and for their integration into society (interview Ehn; *Smålänningen* 21 February 2002, p. 1, 7).

For half of their available time, the participants were occupied with work and given education in Swedish for the remaining half. They were certainly not launched headlong into the programme immediately after arrival; they first had to undergo basic full-time education in Swedish (*Smålänningen* 21 February 2002, p. 1, 7). Most of the participants were from Bosnia and Iraq. 50-60 of them were labelled as newly arrived immigrants, while a further 150 had come to Ljungby during the past two years (*Smålänningen* 21 February 2002, p. 1, 7).

The project turned out to be quite successful. One official at the social security bureau perceived it to be a way out of passivity and welfare dependency. The coordinator of the project exclaimed in the local paper that, finally, the immigrants were being seen as an asset and not a liability (*Smålänningen* 28 May 2002, p. 4). Provided that they committed themselves to the programme, the immigrants were given an introductory grant that was paid by the municipality. The project was to be short-lived however. The head of the social services branch of the municipal government, a powerful local actor, had argued early on that, if it had to be provided for by the regular budget of the social services, he could see no means to carry on with the project (*Smålänningen* 28 May 2002, p. 4). Some weeks later, the news broke that Ljungby's municipality was not inclined to go on paying for the scheme. It could simply not afford to and the project thus had to be terminated (*Smålänningen* 4 July 2002, p. 5). According to several local actors, the municipal assembly's decision had been unanimous and there had not even been a voting procedure preceding the decision (interview Sjöholm). Everyone seemed to be in favour of the project in principle, but the politicians were not willing to go against the leading official's word that it could not be afforded (interviews Olsson, Lindow, Uvebrant). The project coordinator could only deplore the decision as 'strange' as, during the few months since the inception of the programme, every fifth participant had already acquired a permanent job (*Smålänningen* 4 July 2002, p. 5).

There was however to be a happy ending to the story. Since the problem was not in finding political support for the project, the coordinator was urged to apply for funding from the EU European Social Fund within the so-called Objective 3 for EU support measures. Since she was encouraged to do so only four days in advance of the deadline for application, she speedily wrote an application and delivered it to the regional EU branch office in Växjö. She was successful and the programme received funding from the European Social Fund from January 1, 2003, onwards. Moreover, given satisfactory results and situation reports, there was a good chance of obtaining continuous funding during a 3-year-period (interview Ehn).

On the other occasions when integration issues featured in the local newspaper, this was predominantly in connection with active recruitments of personnel to Ljungby. Quite some attention was given to a project which aimed to provide services to those moving into the region, not least to assist their spouses in attaining meaningful employment or occupation. Again, it was seen as a key to success that those migrating from abroad learnt Swedish quickly and effectively upon their arrival. One such article retold the story of a Polish architect who had gained his employment thanks to the project (*Smålänningen* 13 June 2002, p. 7).

Other cases, however, were less successful. *Smålänningen* took up two instances where highly suitable candidates for positions had been found, but other problems had prevented them from taking up their positions. One story was about a Polish otologist who had been headhunted by Ljungby's hospital. Accommodation, however, had turned out to be a bottleneck. The hospital administration had tried to find a suitable flat for him and his family, but had so far had no success. The specialist was sorely needed, as the waiting lists to the otology department were among the longest in the hospital. Over the last few years, the hospital had successfully recruited two radiologists and one ophthalmologist from Poland, but this time the housing problems seemed too hard to surmount (*Smålänningen* 15 October 2002, p. 7).

Another story involved the local football club, Ljungby IF, which was that year in the second division of the Swedish football league. In December, the sports pages announced that the club was about to make its most spectacular recruitment ever as a Serbian defender, who had played 26 games on the Yugoslavian national team, had decided to join the club. At the time the article went to press, he had been residing in Sweden for 2 ½ years (*Smålänningen* 6 December 2002, p. 30). A plan was agreed upon, according to which the player was to work within the health care sector alongside his activities in the football club. This turned out to be easier said than done, however, and a few days after the erstwhile announcement it appeared that the recruitment was in jeopardy, since he lacked a working permit. The leaders of the football club decided to assist him and declared their intention to send an application for a re-inquiry to the Swedish Migration Board (*Smålänningen* 13 December 2002, p. 35). And they seemed to have been successful since, for the next year at least, the defender was still playing on the team.

In summary then, this was the general context for discussions about immigration issues in Ljungby: a few ups and downs, some serious-minded and well-intended efforts to help immigrants along the way to successful integration, but also some under-the-surface prejudice and scattered manifestations of extremist xenophobic activities. On the whole, however, a picture seemed to emerge of tranquil settings with little drama in them. In connection with the general elections in the autumn, however, some undercurrents that were quite adverse to strangers became more visible in the societal discourse. Here, one could find familiar discussions about risks to cherished values. It is therefore revealing, as well as justified, to have a closer look at how the election campaign was dealt with in the local newspaper coverage of Ljungby and its surroundings.

The Elections: The National Meets the Local

On the eve of the elections of 2002, the theme of xenophobia made its way into most Swedish families' living rooms. It attracted nationwide attention as an investigative journalist, equipped with hidden camera and microphone, visited politicians and electoral workers all across Sweden. He caught a shockingly high number of them saying libellous and condescending things about immigrants in Sweden. It should be pointed out that the news programme—*Uppdrag granskning* (approx. translation 'Mission: Scrutiny')—was itself severely criticised for having had a heavy slant in its selection of interviewees, as most of them represented the Conservatives, while only a few represented the Social Democrats and practically no other parties of the national parliament were scrutinised.

As it happened, however, Ljungby was included in the programme, thus opening up for local debate on the theme, as a national parliamentarian representing the Conservatives was a resident of the town. He was one of those who had articulated markedly negative views about immigrants, even though the staff of the programme were said to have included his statements less because of the substance of what he actually said and more because of the pitch of his voice and his mimicry while saying it (*Smålänningen*, 12 September 2002).

Furthermore and most ironically, the same day as the TV show was broadcast, the parliamentarian had published his views in *Smålänningen* on how the policy of integration should be handled in Sweden. Openness had to be combined with firmness and with clearly formulated laws and rules, he argued. He ended his argument in a pointed manner, using sentences and lines of reasoning that were not uncommon in populist vocabulary, and that were also quite recognisable from the local debate around the events simultaneously unfolding in Markaryd: 'The people who come here to build their future in Sweden must understand right away that we do not condone criminality and violence. If they resort to this, the trust given to them has been misused. In that case, they are not welcome to stay on in our Sweden'. This was the familiar guest metaphor being employed all over again, and themes of risk and danger were obviously prevalent in his argumentation. The parliamentarian went on to say that the description only applied to a small minority and that 'ordinary people' were sure to understand this (*Smålänningen* 11 September 2002).

Although the parliamentarian publicly apologised for his slip-ups in front of the camera, and even confessed his shame about certain statements he had made at the time, all of his party associates were not convinced. The district chairman of the Conservatives' Youth League demanded the parliamentarian's immediate resignation from political office, underlining that the youth league advocated liberal policies of immigration (*Smålänningen* 19 September 2002). A few days later, this same chairman was himself assaulted in a video store in central Ljungby, as a drunken customer hit him in the face and called him a 'bloody racist'. Because the chairman had been wearing the Conservative party insignia, he believed that the attacker had linked the incident to the TV show and the slanderous statements made by several Conservative party representatives, among them the parliamentarian in question (*Smålänningen* 20 September 2002).

In the ensuing local debate that was provoked by the TV programme, the local populist party, the Alternative, entered the fray, underscoring its ambiguous stance on matters of immigration and integration. One of the leading representatives of the Ljungby branch of the party, herself an immigrant who later went on to win a seat in the municipal assembly, stated that many of the controversial views about immigrants that had been expressed by the loose-lipped politicians featured in the TV show were justified and true: 'They live in ghettoes, they have many children, they live on social welfare, they do not want to work'. The conclusion of her letter-to-the-editor was less than clear, although it also claimed to lay the blame elsewhere than on the immigrants themselves. Nonetheless, it certainly reinforced the impression that xenophobic sentiments thrived within the Alternative party (*Smålänningen* 13 September 2002).

The Letters-to-the-Editor Section: A Vehement Debate Before the General Elections

Concerning the issue of immigrants, the letters section was probably the site of the local newspaper where events on the national political arena were most clearly translated into the local context. The first time this happened during 2002 was in the early months of the year, in connection with a highly publicised event when a young woman, living in the Swedish city of Uppsala, was shot dead by her own father, who ostensibly tried to defend the honour of the family. The name of the young woman was Fadime Sahindal, and her tragic death received immense attention both within and outside the borders of Sweden. She became a powerful symbol of young immigrant women who were squeezed between the traditional, patriarchal views and sentiments of their families and the emancipating pressures of the new country. In a comment made immediately after the murder, a representative of the women's emergency centre in Ljungby claimed that 'what happened to her [Fadime] might just as well have happened here'. The representative took pains to underline her opinion that violence and oppression against women could be encountered in all cultures, but she also stressed that women from immigrant groups made up the majority of the clients at the emergency centre. Furthermore, she argued that the problem of daughters being harassed by their families was almost exclusively restricted to immigrants (*Smålänningen* 24 January 2003, p. 4).

The case of Fadime was taken up by several writers in the letters-to-the-editor section. One recurring theme was that her murder signified the future of multicultural Sweden. One writer predicted that it would prove to be just a 'mild dress rehearsal' compared to what might actually befall a future Sweden where Islam had taken secure roots and *sharia* laws had become accepted in Swedish judicial bodies (*Smålänningen*, 11 April 2002, p. 22; cf. 26 March 2002, p. 24). Another voice, purportedly belonging to a concerned old-age pensioner, expressed alarm over 'inhabitants of our country who by tradition have other values than what was so far the majority of the Swedish people' and who therefore were 'prone to commit rape and honour killings'. The writer envisaged that s/he soon would have to lock her-/himself up indoors in order not to be 'mugged or beaten up or maybe murdered' by immigrant youth gangs (*Smålänningen* 25 July 2002, p. 22). A prolific letter writer, with ties to a xenophobic fringe party, asked polemically whether one really deserved to be branded as a 'racist' just because one was opposed to 'imams who wish to cut peoples' throats or bury women from the waist down in the ground and then stone them to death' (*Smålänningen* 16 May 2002, p. 21).

The really big issue on the letter pages, however, concerned the actual costs of immigration for the national Swedish economy. This discussion should definitely be seen in the context of the 2002 general elections, where immigration issues were high on the national agenda. The elections therefore provided the backdrop of what turned out to be a heated local debate devoted to immigration issues in the letters section of *Smålänningen*. In what seemed to be a concerted action, one writer asked to be enlightened by other readers concerning 'the true costs' of immigration for the Swedish taxpayer. He said that he had seen as diverging estimates as 30 billion and 250 billion Swedish kronor per annum (*Smålänningen* 21 May 2002, p. 15). In a letter about three weeks later, another writer advocated the higher figure, arguing that the Swedish government had 'put the lid on the discussion' so that the public would not 'interfere', and if somebody still did, he or she could always be written off as 'racist or xenophobic' (*Smålänningen* 12 June 2002, p. 23; also 26 June 2002, p. 26).

In early July, one letter writer claimed to be able to provide an answer to the original question, referring to a book by a certain Lars Jansson, purportedly a lecturer at Gothenburg University. (A search in the Gothenburg University staff directory failed to reveal anyone with that name and position.) In the book, the total costs of immigration were estimated to be 267 billion kronor per annum for the Swedish national economy. According to the writer, Jansson's claim was that the costs had tripled during the last decade of the 20th century. The skyrocketing costs, the argument continued, had to be borne by the Swedish public through cuts in expenditure on health care, education, law and order, communications and old age pensions *(Smålänningen* 4 July 2002, p. 20). Jansson himself entered the debate some weeks later, largely repeating the allegations *(Smålänningen,* 23 July 2002). He maintained that the economic benefits offered by the state made Sweden an attractive country of immigration, and that less than 10 per cent of those received as asylum-seekers had legitimate reasons for asylum. To be sure, most of them were moving away from poverty and unemployment, but they could not be regarded as refugees. According to Jansson, the Swedish government and its 'supporting parties' amounted to 'the best friends of the human smugglers' in Europe, most of who were 'foreigners or former foreigners' (the latter is indeed a revealing term—once a foreigner, always a foreigner!). Finally, he claimed that the 600 000 immigrants that did after all have jobs in Sweden still squeezed out Swedish welfare and put downward pressure on wages for those who were already poorly paid *(Smålänningen* 20 August 2002, p. 21). According to writers holding similar views, the responsibility for the all-too-liberal Swedish immigration policies had a face, namely the then Minister for Integration, Ms. Mona Sahlin *(Smålänningen* 25 September 2002, p. 26). As one writer chose to phrase it, the current policies were the fault of 'Mona Sahlin and her like-minded Social Acrobats' *(Smålänningen* 15 August 2002, p. 22).

The national pre-election debate of 2002 was to a large extent dominated by the People's Party, a liberal party traditionally associated with a generous outlook on policies of immigration and asylum, as well as on issues such as international developmental aid. During the summer of 2002, the party leader Lars Leijonborg made a partial volte-face, as he started to argue that welfare benefits had to be combined with demands made on immigrants. He suggested for instance that citizenship be made contingent on a minimum threshold of knowledge of the Swedish language. Certain minimum achievements in linguistic tests should become a criterion for being granted Swedish citizenship, he argued. Critics claimed that the message was hard to combine with the liberal views normally associated with the People's Party, and held that the party was trying to exploit sombre xenophobic sentiments. The electorate, however, responded positively to the reorientation of the party, which had remarkable success at the polls.

The pros and cons of linguistic tests thus came to constitute a part of the debate in the letters section. Jansson, for one, saw the merits in the suggestion, even though he thought that it was 'banal' and that it was made 30 years too late. He thought it noteworthy that, despite its 'innocence', it had caused an 'uproar in the media and among politicians, especially on the left wing'. All in all, he held it to be 'self-evident' that not only citizenship but also permanent residence permits had to be made contingent on linguistic skills. In all, he went markedly further than the People's Party had done in their call for such tests *(Smålänningen* 20 August 2002, p. 21). Other writers, too, praised the perceived reorientation of the People's Party, even though they also characterised it as repentance in the nick of time *(Smålänningen* 6 August 2002, p. 15; 15 August 2002, p. 22). In one letter, Leijonborg was advised to study the policies advocated by the leader of the populist Danish People's Party, Pia Kjaersgaard, if he had not done so already (*Smålänningen* 6 August 2002, p. 15). Indeed, this was not the only time that Kjaersgaard was invoked as a fitting role model for Swedish politicians to take after (*Smålänningen* 4 June 2002, p. 21; 29 July 2002, p. 15). One letter writer, purportedly an old-age retiree, half-jokingly suggested that, in view of the developments he perceived in Swedish society, it was probably time for him to start thinking seriously about applying for political asylum in Denmark (*Smålänningen* 25 July, 2002, p. 22).

During the summer of 2002, champions of liberal ideas on immigration countered this onslaught and rallied to defend their values on the letters page. One writer argued that immigration had, on balance and seen in a historical perspective, been a profitable affair for the Swedish national economy. It was only in the 1990s, when Swedish asylum policies turned more restrictive, he went on to argue, that it started to become unprofitable for the state. After this turn, refugees had been gathered into reception camps, where they were not permitted to work during a lengthy period of inquiry. Even so, he held, Jansson's figures were grossly exaggerated (*Smålänningen* 11 July 2002, p. 21). The lower figure of 30 billion kronor per annum was defended by the writer, with references made to a study by (what this time actually was) a well-known professor at Växjö University (*Smålänningen*, 11 July 2002, p. 21; 21 August 2002, p. 23).

The same writer went so far as to accuse *Smålänningen* of allowing xenophobic forces to use the letters page to articulate their views and to spread lies about immigration (*Smålänningen* 11 July 2002, p. 21). This prompted the editor-in-chief to enter the melee and argue that the accuser had proceeded from the false premises that all criticism against Swedish policies of immigration was driven by racism and xenophobia. Rather, he said, it should be seen as a sign of the good health of an open debate that the arena provided by the local newspaper even allowed for controversial issues to be discussed (*Smålänningen* 11 July 2002, p. 21). Here one can question the extent to which the editor was actually defending views that he really wished to defend, or whether he was simply defending journalistic principles. Like other editors in similar situations, he may have felt under pressure to protect the principle of free expression, even though the ideas may have run contrary to his own convictions (cf. Wahl-Jorgensen 2004:94). At any rate, his intervention as well as his timing of it seemed unfortunate.

A Green Party representative of Ljungby's municipal assembly subsequently joined the discussion. She asked rhetorically why immigrants did not get the jobs they applied for and, if they did, why their wages were so much lower than the majority population's. The current treatment of asylum-seekers risked giving rise to covert everyday racism, she argued, and went on to say that current policies of immigration were not very successful, characterised as they were by both inhumanity and red tape (*Smålänningen*, 8 August 2002, p. 13). She claimed that the current political debate on achievements in linguistic tests as a criterion for gaining citizenship smacked of intolerance, and that 'Swedishness' on dubious grounds was being elevated into the position of a norm (*Smålänningen* 30 August 2002, p. 23). In a counter-response to the aforementioned adherents of much more restrictive views, she retorted concerning Jansson's oft-cited study that 'stupidities do not become less stupid just because someone has written them down in a book'. She held that the arguments forwarded by Jansson seemed to be based on a rejection of the principle of the equal worth of all human beings and hinted that Jansson 'may himself be a bearer and a multiplier of the discriminatory attitudes that make it so hard for immigrants and refugees to become integrated in Swedish society' (*Smålänningen* 30 August 2002, p. 23).

After this forceful intervention the Green Party assembly member seemed to have been given the final word. There was a belated response, almost a month later, in which her merits for questioning the proclaimed authority and the 'lifelong scholarly education' of Lars Jansson were cast doubt upon (*Smålänningen* 25 September 2002, p. 26; cf. *Smålänningen* 26 August 2002, p. 23). However, by all appearances, the debate on the costs of immigration ended, at least for the rest of the year.

It deserves to be pointed out that many letters did not make it to the pages of the newspaper. According to the editor-in-chief of *Smålänningen*, several letters were thrown into the dustbin since they expressed purely racist views. They were quite simply not fit to print (interview Gustafsson). Even so, as has been shown, the bulk of those letters that did make it through the gate were already in themselves quite derogatory in tone and substance, and thus taken together they probably served to entrench negative stereotypes among the readers.

Stereotyping the Strangers

There were thus visible undercurrents on the letters-to-the-editor page that indicated that several segments of *Smålänningen's* readership were at the very least cautious about immigrants. Of course, there is no way of telling whether the writers of the letters were inhabitants of the municipality of Ljungby as such. In order to be able to say more about the sentiments in Ljungby as reflected in *Smålänningen*, we have to turn to the news coverage of what took place in the town itself during the year in question. As already mentioned, in assessing the news pages, we have to bear in mind the fact that the old idealised view of articles as faithfully and objectively reporting reality is outdated. Reality is never objective, as it is always perceived through the eyes of someone. The act of news reporting is based on subjective choices made by both editors and journalists and it is also affected by the media logic of operation. Selection and framing are not givens but are crucial elements of a construction process that will impact on the further moulding of the perceptions of the readers. Indeed, this is why processes such as stereotype-formation are so important to study and analyse.

As was argued in the introductory chapters, stereotypes of perceived foreigners and strangers need not be pronouncedly negative or indicate malevolent traits on the part of their objects to have an overall negative effect. For, if they are not negative, they tend to be romanticising, which can be just as harmful to possibilities for integration. *Smålänningen's* news reporting revealed several examples of both negative and romanticising stereotypes during the year. Russia and Eastern Europe were the geographical areas that featured most frequently and prominently in the stereotypes that were constructed about foreign peoples and countries. In one rather bizarre example, one could for instance read that the cases of people being infested by lice had increased in Sweden, as more Swedish tourists travelled to and from Eastern Europe and the former Soviet Union (*Smålänningen* 23 January 2002, p. 8). On the other hand, one could also read that the peoples of the Baltic states of Estonia, Latvia and Lithuania were generally 'very hospitable' and easy to get along with (*Smålänningen* 19 February 2002, p. 8)—seemingly the kind of clichés often encountered in travellers' handbooks. A female high school student from Ljungby was not so complimentary, however, in a letter she wrote to *Smålänningen* during her third year in Moscow. Her impression from the airport was that the terminal was 'an unbelievably ugly building painted in a dirty brownish colour'. Inside it 'Russian women swaggered past wearing green military jackets and short skirts', talking in a language from which she could only pick up 'a lot of consonants and ssshh-sounds in an incomprehensible order' (*Smålänningen* 3 April 2002, p. 18-19). Not to be deterred however, other high school students from Ljungby reported back from a visit to Gdansk in Poland that they had been able to see for themselves that everything was not painted in 'communist grey'. One student held that he thought that Poland would eventually catch up with Sweden in all respects. That is to say that it was certainly not deemed to be there as of yet (*Smålänningen* 11 September 2002, p. 6).

The 'lagging behind' factor was prevalent in many descriptions pertaining to Russia and Eastern Europe. The Moscow-based student reported for instance that 'Moscow is quite a bit behind in its development if one compares it with a city in Sweden' (*Smålänningen* 3 April 2002, p. 18-19). With regard to international projects conducted within the EU frame, involving Russia as well as the then applicant countries in Central Eastern Europe, the role of helper was frequently attributed to Sweden, while the applicant countries and Russia were depicted to be on the receiving end. This applied among other things to areas such as waste disposal, environmental protection and the recycling of goods (*Smålänningen* 24 July 2002, p. 5; 9 October 2002, p. 8). Peoples of the eastern part of Europe were often described as the clients in a patronage relation. The contexts varied and could for instance pertain to the reception of Belorussian children in a summer camp outside Ljungby (*Smålänningen* 19 August 2002, p. 4) or to the Christmas donations of discarded clothes, shoes and toys to a Lithuanian town (*Smålänningen* 24 December 2002, p. 9).

As already mentioned, romanticising stereotypes could also be found. Regarding features perceived as exotic, one representative of a group of Transylvanian folk dancers was quoted as saying: 'The dance and Transylvania are inseparable. There are dances for all kinds of mood. We dance when we are happy and we dance when we are sad' (*Smålänningen* 25 February 2002, p. 6). Similar images were conveyed about members of the Hungarian society in Ljungby (*Smålänningen* 1 October 2002, p. 18).

Perpetrators of Crime

Aside from these tendencies to stereotype representatives of certain foreign countries, there were also two genre-based stereotypes in the news reporting, which are well-known in other literature in the field (e.g. Brune 2002, Haavisto 2002). They were constructed and conveyed through the news reports about asylum-seekers, refugees and foreign people in general. I am referring to the two broadly stereotyped categories of immigrants as perpetrators and of immigrants as victims. As we shall see, these stereotypes are constructed not so much through explicit references to the essentialised characteristics of certain groups, as they are implied through the frequent mentioning of immigrants, most often refugees and asylum-seekers in certain news contexts.

We have already seen how the 2002 events in Markaryd were reported in *Smålänningen*. Among readers already prone to associate refugees and asylum-seekers with disorder and crime, the effect of this series of articles was, in all likelihood, to further entrench these beliefs. Ljungby did not experience anything like this kind of turbulence, which is maybe no big surprise since, unlike Markaryd, there was no reception centre for asylum-seekers in the municipality. All the same, images were conveyed by the news reports, according to which immigrants were associated with different manifestations of socio-cultural risk.

As noted in Chapter 5, the policy of *Smålänningen* is not to publish any details about the ethnicity of perpetrators of crime, unless it adds something substantial to the understanding of the case. Even so, there were some incidents reported on in the newspaper which, added together, could be taken by readers so inclined as evidence of the general criminal disposition of immigrant strangers. To cite one such example, it was reported in May that a woman living on her own in a rural area had had her jewellery stolen by a gang of foreign criminals. Apparently, this gang had chosen to concentrate their activities on the countryside and the single, elderly people living there. The victim had been visited by four adults and an infant, and the grown-ups had reportedly begged her for 'latte' and 'bread' for the baby (*Smålänningen* 22 May 2002, p. 5). In connection with what seemed to be the same gang, the readers of an article a few days later were warned not to forget to bolt their doors and not to let in people unknown to them. The reason was that the Ljungby region had become a base of operations for a group of 'travelling thieves' in cars with 'foreign license-plates'. If discovered, this 'group of travellers' had a tactic to divert attention; by throwing an infant into the arms of the person in the process of catching them, they used the resulting disarray to flee (*Smålänningen* 28 May 2002, p. 7).

In addition, on the Ljungby pages of *Smålänningen* there was a handful of articles throughout the year where details either spelling out or implying the ethnicity of perpetrators of crimes were provided. Thus, even though the readers could hardly draw the conclusion that all crimes were committed by immigrants, they could still potentially read the information as confirming their prejudice that a relatively large part of immigrants in Sweden had a criminal disposition and were involved in crime. This risk was enhanced by the fact that most articles about immigrants and foreigners tended to portray them either as perpetrators or victims. Indeed, what was lacking was articles depicting them in mundane, everyday situations, just like the proverbial you and me.

Regarding the travelling gang of thieves referred to above, there were several expressions and subtle signs conveyed in the article that indicated them to be a group of Roma people. The rationale for revealing such details seemed to be to warn the public, lest other, similar acts be committed in the neighbourhood. In the same category, one could place an article about a 'foreign-looking' attempted rapist, who remained at large in Ljungby and who, it was feared, would attack again unless apprehended (*Smålänningen* 23 October 2002, p. 1, 5).

There were, however, several examples of unnecessary and unwarranted details being given about ethnic origin in other cases. This included the story of a man of East European origin who had committed car thefts in the Ljungby area and had stated a false identity when he was caught (*Smålänningen* 4 March 2002, p. 6), that of a group of Lithuanians involved in a burglary tour of the region (*Smålänningen* 10 October, p. 3; 11 December, p. 5), another about Romanian tourists who were caught with a lot of burglary loot in their car (*Smålänningen* 4 July 2002, p. 1, 4), yet another about a German couple who had been swindling camp site owners and private landlords for substantial amounts of money (*Smålänningen* 23 October, p. 5) and finally one about a shoplifter in Ljungby, who had lost his temper and threatened a guard who had caught him in the act and addressed him as 'bin Laden' (*Smålänningen* 21 November 2002, p. 6).

Again, even if *Smålänningen* was relatively restrictive in revealing details about the ethnic backgrounds of perpetrators of crime of different magnitudes, the number of articles that did get through with such information were probably enough to entrench negative stereotypes about strangers, immigrants and refugees. This was even more so when seen in conjunction with the events that were being reported from Markaryd. On top of this, representatives of the regional police force stated that they were not able to combat the growing influx of drugs to Ljungby as the refugee reception centres in the neighbouring municipality tied up too much of their resources (*Smålänningen* 29 May 2002, p. 1, 4). Added to the multitude of other reports that were emanating from the nearby municipality, this was fairly likely to create an accumulated effect among those who were already critical to the presence of immigrants and refugees in Ljungby and its surroundings.

More than any other geographical area, Eastern Europe and the former Soviet Union were depicted as breeding grounds for criminals, who were subsequently finding their way to Sweden. Other areas of origin were not depicted in an equally straightforward manner. The tendency to single out the region was indicated, not only by the string of cases recounted above, but was also rather bluntly stated by a police officer, who told *Smålänningen* that there were two main categories of burglaries that were currently affecting Ljungby. The first category consisted of crimes committed by desperate and disoriented drug addicts, who destroyed almost everything in their way. The second one, however, consisted of groups 'from the former communist states in the East. They do not destroy as much [as the aforementioned category] and they steal almost exclusively money and jewellery.... They pocket the money directly and they send the trinkets on by regular mail...' (*Smålänningen* 10 July 2002, p. 36).

The Victims

Portraying immigrants as hapless victims might sometimes be for commendable purposes and may also have positive effects for the individual thus depicted. The journalist writing the story may wish to stir up a discussion, increase societal commitment or prompt bureaucrats into action. The flipside of the coin is that categories of groups and individuals who are frequently portrayed as victims are also likely to be attributed some kind of inferiority and childlike vulnerability. If people thus categorised are not seen to be protected by their stronger betters, it will be perceived as a risk that they could be led astray into crime, or else that they might simply be lost in the hostile world 'out there'. This can be summarised as the logic behind the application of the dual set of stereotypes found in the nexus between the victim and the perpetrator.

We have seen above how certain countries and peoples in Eastern Europe and Russia were consistently depicted as being weaker than Sweden and the Swedes. They were seen as laggards, who might in some cases catch up at a later stage, but certainly not in the near future. Concerning the admittedly very rare examples when peoples from developing countries in the so-called 'Third World' were written about, the underlying position of weakness was made even clearer. A telling example of this tendency was provided by the story of a Swedish missionary (a relic from the 1980s!) representing the Pentecostal Church in Ljungby, who had hosted some Bolivian Indian children for a few weeks in the winter. On visiting a school, the children had reportedly been 'overwhelmed' by the multitude of chairs and tables in the classrooms (*Smålänningen*, 19 February 2002, p. 8).

As for foreign nationals who came to Sweden and Ljungby to settle, there were a few cases where the conveyed position of weakness and the depicted need for protection came through very clearly. Let me recount three principal stories that ran during the year. In early 2002, there was an article about a Turkish resident of Ljungby who had his teenaged nephew and niece staying with him. Their parents had died and so, for some time, they had been taken care of by their grandfather and grandmother in Turkey but, as these were now ailing and could not support them, they had moved to their uncle in Sweden. According to decisions by the Swedish Migration Board and the Aliens Appeals Board, the two teenagers had to be evicted from Sweden. One of the reasons provided for the decisions was that they had never shared a common household with their uncle during their years in Turkey. Also, they had come to Sweden without valid visa or residence permits. If evicted, they faced an uncertain future, with the possibilities of crime and prostitution reported as potential last resorts to support themselves. There was some local support for their cause. The principal of their school in Ljungby spoke out on their behalf, arguing that they had 'blended in incredibly well' (*Smålänningen* 19 February, p. 1, 4.) Later in the year, there was a new development in the case, as the uncle filed an application to legally adopt the children. The resolution of the case was not reported, but the signs were hopeful (*Smålänningen* 5 March 2002, p. 7).

The second case was very tragic. It concerned a family of Kosovo Albanians who resided in the region. They had repeatedly applied for a residence permit in Sweden, but had had their request turned down eight times over. They had been staying in a nearby refugee reception centre in the town of Alvesta since 1998, but had lately chosen to stay at secret addresses, moving around to evade eviction. Sympathetic helpers provided them with food and shelter. The woman in the family had undergone medical treatment for psychiatric problems and had apparently lost her will to live. The children were also reportedly in very bad condition. A local person acting on their behalf underlined that this was a 'decent family who really wished to work and take care of its own subsistence' (*Smålänningen* 13 June 2002, p. 1, 20-21). In the autumn, however, things turned from bad to worse. Through a go-between, the mother of the family made contact with *Smålänningen* and volunteered for an interview to throw light on their situation. She was desperate, after having lived under cover for seven months. As the journalist arrived at the agreed meeting place, she had already tried to commit suicide by taking an overdose of pills. The journalist was not able to get any response from her, and she was acutely taken by ambulance to the emergency ward in Ljungby (*Smålänningen* 6 November 2002, p. 1, 4).

The third story was most of all one about the failure of the Swedish welfare state. However, as in the case just recounted, this story could also be read as an example that provided an exception to the rule that most immigrants had come to Sweden to take advantage of the welfare system. For as we saw, a well-meaning friend assured the local readership that the Kosovan family really wished to work and take care of its own subsistence. Similarly, in the third case dealt with on the Ljungby pages, an elderly couple originating from Yugoslavia told their sad story, while the journalist underlined that they had never wished to be a burden to Swedish society. They had arrived in Sweden more than 30 years ago, both with solid educations. Throughout their active careers, they had worked and supported themselves; the only grant they had received from the municipality was child allowance. The husband had had a stroke more than nine years ago, and he had never completely recovered. He was tended to by his wife, but she had now developed cancer and no longer had the strength to take care of him. They had consequently requested a service flat designed for the disabled and elderly but, so far, this had been denied to them by the municipality (*Smålänningen* 14 August 2002, p. 4).

This particular article may very well fit into the category where the journalist tries to fulfil a worthy purpose by writing the piece, namely, to prompt the municipal authorities into taking the desired action. Here, the newspaper is not only a mirror of societal events (as argued by the editors of *Smålänningen*) but is also, and above all, a powerful societal actor. Still, one has to be highly critical of the tacitly implied idea in this story that most *other* immigrants to Sweden abuse the welfare system and that people, such as the elderly couple from Yugoslavia, constitute exceptions to the rule. Such implied messages serve only to consolidate prevailing stereotypical beliefs that the bulk of immigrants constitute a burden to society. And so, while positive net effects can be achieved in the individual case, for the group as a whole the long-term price is high.

Imminent Threats to Cherished Values?

When a community closes ranks against outsiders, the grounds for doing so can differ widely. Those who are on the margins may be relegated to this position because of their perceived inability to adapt to prevailing interpretations of national identity and preferred cultural mores. But they can also be given the cold shoulder because of perceived incongruity with local and regional patterns of belonging. The boundaries between the different domains and levels of belonging are fuzzy and, in practice, it makes little difference whether outlandishness is perceived in relation to local, regional or national communities. Still, regardless of the level of belonging that is cherished, the net effect of insiders asserting such boundaries to protect their we-community is likely to be one where the outsiders are branded as strange and foreign.

Manifestations of nationalism were few in Ljungby, but assertions of local and regional identities were enough to produce adversity vis-à-vis strangers. Indeed, after following the reporting of *Smålänningen* during a year, it became quite clear that Ljungby is a town with a clearly exhibited local identity. Interviewees testified that Ljungby was a close-knit community, into which it was difficult to force one's way. Even those who had moved in from other parts of the country several years ago and happened to have purportedly 'Swedish-sounding' names, found it hard to become fully accepted[1]. One interviewee had moved into the town in the 1970s but still found herself to be mainly socialising with others who had also moved in from the outside (interview Aspman-Walleij). Several interviewees referred to a special 'Ljungby spirit of mind'.

The examples of majority-minority relations and the construction of local identity recounted above are all fairly non-dramatic and amounted at most to low-level irritants. No major threats towards ingrained and cherished values could be discerned on the Ljungby news pages. As we have seen, the letters page told a partly different story, bearing witness to undercurrents that did not surface elsewhere in the paper. Indeed, there was only one instance when perceived threats to locally cherished values were explicitly spelt out on the Ljungby news pages. The occasion was in early November, when the traditional and low-key Swedish All Saints' Day ritual of lighting candles by the headstones of one's loved ones had, in recent years, been met with competition from the simultaneous and substantially louder Halloween celebrations, largely inspired by American cultural practices and heavily supported by local tradesmen. The parish priest in Ljungby was not amused. He believed the Halloween celebrations to be a fad, merely a transient phenomenon, but stressed that elderly people took offence when they had to meet 'ghosts, skeletons and witches' on their way to the cemetery (*Smålänningen* 31 October 2002, p. 20-21).

Some attention was also given to a long-term trend that had been discerned over a number of years, which featured strangers of a traditional and familiar nature. A substantial number of cottages and leisure houses in the area had in recent years been bought by foreign citizens, above all by Danes but also to some extent by German and Dutch citizens. These nationalities also formed the bulk of foreign tourists in the municipality. On the county level, 320 cottages had switched owners during the year of 1999 and, of those, 60 per cent were purchased by Danes (*Smålänningen* 8 August 2002, p. 7). Indeed, 2002 experienced some kind of all time high regarding demand on the cottage market. The weak standing of the Swedish krona together with the recent opening of the Öresund Bridge between Sweden and Denmark made real estate in the Ljungby region readily accessible to Danish buyers. The car ride from Copenhagen to Ljungby now took only two and a half hours to complete. A local estate agent remarked that he had never experienced anything like it: real estate sold almost immediately and the sky seemed to be the limit when it came to prices. The demand was highest for objects located in isolated, wooded areas. Prices for such dwellings had doubled in two years. Still, the real-estate agent could not see any problems with the fact that cottages and leisure houses increasingly 'fell into foreign hands'. This, he maintained, was a better alternative to leaving them unoccupied to decay. As he saw it, the new owners brought new life to the countryside (*Smålänningen* 16 August 2002, p. 1, 4).

All this aside, the town of Ljungby did also seem prepared to welcome strangers and influences from further afield than Denmark, Germany and Holland. In the autumn, *Smålänningen* (16 October 2002, p. 8) recounted how a shoemaker, who had arrived as a refugee from Bosnia in the early 1990s, had now moved into 'an old, traditional shoemaker's setting' and opened a shoe shop in the centre. The fact that the local newspaper chose to inform its readers about the event certainly seemed to indicate that this was a rather spectacular thing to happen. In another example and in connection with the Ljungby fair in the late summer, the town-dwellers had the chance to acquaint themselves with different cuisines, and the local newspaper did its best to stress the mixture between the accustomed and the exotic: 'Pancakes, Russian pastries and kebab. Herring, Indian food and pasta. Langos, cous cous and Asian food. Grilled pike and hamburger.' A chef from one of the Asian restaurants in the town stressed the opportunity to test Asian food as an alternative to the traditional, local sausage (*Smålänningen* 15 August 2002, p. 18-19). And perhaps this food fest can be seen as symbolic for the level of development towards multiculturalism that had so far been reached in Ljungby; it had still not moved beyond an increasing openness towards probing 'exotic' flavours and cuisines from foreign countries. There was a considerable way to go before it could be said that the immigrants were beginning to become truly integrated, and thus natural and invisible, components of the absolutely normal life of the town. In this sense, they were still absent from the everyday.

Concluding the Case: Socio-Cultural Risk in Ljungby

The events in Ljungby and Markaryd during 2002, as mirrored in the local newspaper, were of course widely dissimilar in a number of ways. Developments in Ljungby were nowhere close to the drama that unfolded in the neighbouring municipality. Aside from this statement of the obvious, however, some more interesting differences could also be found, concerning the actual reporting in *Smålänningen*. As we have seen, in the Markaryd case, there was a marked polarisation in the community discourse between the settled majority, on the one hand, and the residents of the reception centre for asylum-seekers, on the other. For the majority population, societal values were challenged by the inmates of the asylum-seeker camp who, in the newspaper reporting, were portrayed as part of a rather homogeneous mass of 'asylum-seekers'. Detailed information about the ethnicity or national origin of perceived wrongdoers or perpetrators was seldom disclosed by the paper and so the stage seemed to be set, somewhat paradoxically and despite all original good intentions, for tensions to rise between the settled majority and the collectivity of asylum-seekers as a whole. The entire category of asylum-seekers was made suspect, all depicted as if they, without exception, posed a threat to the societal values, property and indeed physical well-being of the local population.

Since there was no compound for asylum-seekers in Ljungby, the residents of this small-town seemed instead to fight their battles against the world 'out there'. For although there did not seem to be a similar need to discern scapegoats for societal shortcomings as there was in Markaryd, there were still deemed to be some, however vague, risks stemming from an increasingly mobile and assertive international environment that needed to be accounted for. And these risks were seen to have a discernible origin. According to the reporting in *Smålänningen,* most of them emanated from Eastern Europe and the former Soviet Union. There were several cases when perpetrators of, most often petty, crimes were revealed to originate from this part of the world. In an otherwise relatively harmonious setting, there was an evident suspicion geared in this direction. The stories that were told clearly designated the region as a hotbed of trouble, full of potential threats to traditional ways of living.

The public narratives in Ljungby that were retold in and by the local newspaper seemed to represent contradicting discourses. On the one hand, public battles were fought to thwart the spectres of racism, xenophobia and intolerance. Indeed, Ljungby did not suffer from the presence of any vigilante movements directed at strangers. Instead, the municipality had well-intended and positive programmes designed to integrate immigrants into community life, at least to such a degree that they could gain temporary jobs and basic education in the Swedish language. According to the official line, the manufacturing industry still provided an outlet for immigrant workers. Racism was conveniently located elsewhere. Nonetheless, Ljungby was a tightly-knit community to fight its way into, and it was still considered big news when occasional immigrants made it and thus could represent a token story of success. They were cast in the role of the exceptions that proved 'the rule' that the bulk of the immigrants otherwise ended up as perpetrators of crime, or as victims that needed to be taken care of by society and thus constituted a burden for the taxpaying majority. Regardless however of whether the immigrants ended up as perpetrators or victims, they were believed to connote a fair share of socio-cultural risk. The pre-election debate in the letters section amply revealed such sentiments, even if it is of course unclear to what extent it was orchestrated by the locals of Ljungby itself.

This chapter started with an excursion back in time, to the late 1980s. Judging from the reporting that took place then, it was above all the exoticising stereotypes that were used in the news coverage. The newcomers came from exotic countries, cooked exotic food, and made different kinds of exotic manifestations of culture. On top of this, there was the seemingly anachronistic, openly colonial and missionary outlook on the 'Third World' as being in dire need of salvation and basic education. At the same time, there was less discussion about the risks and threats brought about by these newcomers, as other demons seemed to be haunting the townspeople, above all the HIV/Aids pandemic and different symptoms of environmental degradation. The residents of Ljungby in 1987 did not therefore seem to worry overly much about risks brought by immigrants, even though the letters section also then contained occasional comments about the immigrants connoting a straining financial burden. Nor was there really any talk of racism. However, there was an island mentality where the bridge-building metaphor was often fittingly used. Bridges had to be built between the 'Swedes' and the 'immigrants', but once these brief meetings between the two essentialised categories had taken place, the bridges crumbled once again, and the groups went on to lead their separate lives.

The immigrants were certainly not part of everyday life in 1987. Nor were they part of it in 2002. The foremost difference between the two periods seemed to be that, whereas they used to be regarded as exotic and were thus excluded from community life on those grounds, they were now increasingly seen as risky and threatening, and were not allowed to be part of the everyday for that reason. But it was, for all practical purposes, the same old exclusion at work.

Notes

1. This example can be compared to the general wariness about outsiders that is described in Norman's (2004:211) nicknamed village of Gruvbo.

7. Urban Legends and False Rumours: Pizzerias in Älmhult

Not many scholars are given the honour of having societal phenomena named after them, but the Swedish ethnologist Bengt af Klintberg is one of the few. In the mid-1980s, he published a bestselling book about folklore myths that have been told and retold in our contemporary times. They tell the stories of incredible, absurd, bizarre and scary events, and as a rule the narrators swear them to be true. All of the stories have been heard from reliable sources, they claim, either from the friend of a friend, acquaintances or authoritative persons. The events are all said to have taken place at specified locations, so that the place and the time of the event are provided with great accuracy (Klintberg 1990:8). The stories travel, across countries and continents, with new locations and temporal definitions pegged to them every time. In Sweden, these travelling folklore myths have been labelled 'Klintberg stories' in colloquial language. In English, there are other terms, like urban folk tales, urban legends, urban myths and contemporary legends (Dingwall 2001). The most internationally known analyst and re-teller of these myths is the ethnologist Jan Harold Brunvand (1981, 1984), who has also proved a great source of inspiration for Klintberg.

According to Klintberg (1990:9-10), the travelling myths bear witness to beliefs and values that are prevalent in our times. They constitute 'collective fantasies which reflect the worldviews of their time'. Above all, they deal with subjects experienced as troubling by common people in their everyday lives, such as those phenomena that are perceived as unknown, strange and therefore threatening. And even if not all or even the majority of these folklore myths deal with immigrants and other kinds of perceived strangers, several of them do. They thus serve to reinforce stereotyped beliefs and further accentuate the marginalisation of depicted groups. Dingwall (2001:192) observes that the stories allow the re-tellers to communicate their concerns in ways that otherwise would not have been acceptable or would even have been stigmatised. Through the narrating mechanisms and the format of urban legends, it is possible for the narrator to transgress the borderlines of what would otherwise have been regarded as improper. S/he will not even be required to phrase the standard mantra of 'I am not a racist, but…'; simply retelling what one has heard will permit the orator to articulate her/his view anyway.

The travelling myths convey the picture of a society that is beleaguered by perceived dangers and perils. Klintberg (1990:10) makes the observation that a common denominator of all of the myths is that they are all fundamentally about ways in which the privileged West senses various kinds of threat as emanating from a 'Third World' that is perceived as wild, unchained and demanding. Thus, travelling myths tie in well with the general argument that stereotypes are a mode of maintaining the boundaries between Us and Them. By depicting the Others as bizarre, strange, irrational or threatening, the We can entrench its feelings of its own perceived excellence and superiority.

Even though urban legends are not necessarily or even most typically a small-town phenomenon, they may well thrive in such a setting. They may, for instance, serve to add some spice to a day-to-day rhythm, where nothing out of the ordinary ever seems to happen (Dingwall 2001:186). And even more importantly, they can be seen as building blocks of everyday life, laying a foundation to protect it from outside disturbances. There is often a clear morality that is added to the stories, and they serve to issue clear normative recommendations regarding proper ways of action. The very fact that they are reiterated in different settings can be seen as deriving from the 'imperturbability of the mundane world' and of everyday life itself (Dingwall 2001: 194-195). The relative lack of drama in everyday existence may at times be perceived as unexciting but, while it is no doubt challenged by the phenomena recounted in the myths, the everyday routine is actually as much safeguarded by the internal mechanisms and format of the story-telling phenomenon. The strange and the stranger reappear as deviant and threatening but there is a familiarity and regularity in these qualities. They are somehow transformed into the devil you already know.

Why Talk About Pizzerias?

Not so many decades ago, pizzerias constituted the quintessential token of the new and challenging times ahead facing the Swedish countryside. Previously, restaurants serving traditional Swedish food had reigned more or less supreme. Even though their menus were rather unexciting at times, they were deemed to be reliable and familiar by their customers. I can recall that when the first pizzeria was established in my own home town, in the early 1970s, my parents' generation was deeply sceptical. Today, this kind of reaction would be considered to be a thing of the past. Indeed, in most Swedish rural small-towns, one is now hard put to find a restaurant that is not a pizzeria or a Chinese restaurant.

The pizzeria phenomenon is neither new nor exciting any more, and one would no longer tend to think of it as a symbol of the perceived new and strange. Or, at least, so it would seem.

Given some afterthought, however, it may still symbolise, if not the strange, then at least the strangers. Whereas the Swedish labour market is frequently rigid and ungenerous towards highly qualified and specialised contenders from abroad, the pizzerias have, together with fast-food joints and taxi companies, provided one of the rare outlets. A former Swedish Minister of Integration, Ms. Mona Sahlin, exclaimed on one occasion that she was sick and tired of 'riding taxis driven by [immigrant] doctors and buying hamburgers from engineers' (*Aftonbladet* 22 October 2000). Sahlin made this statement in order to legitimise her suggestion that affirmative action be considered in Swedish labour legislation, to make it easier for immigrants to obtain jobs for which they had already acquired qualified education and practical skills in their countries of origin. And to be sure, the examples she drew upon were widely known to the Swedish public. She spoke about a reality to which many could relate. By way of illustration, a municipal commissioner of Ljungby remarked that 'had it not been for the immigrants, there would have been no pizzerias in the town' (interview Bengtsson). The conclusions that this interviewee drew from the observation were not necessarily the same as those arrived at by Ms. Sahlin, but the awareness was surely still there that this was a line of business dominated by immigrants.

Thus, for many people in Sweden, pizzerias can be seen as a location for strangers, even though the phenomenon as such can hardly any more be said to epitomise the strange. It is against this background that we should view the rather bizarre events and discussions that emanated from the town of Älmhult in 2002 and which were reflected by the local newspaper, *Smålänningen.*

Rumour in Älmhult

Älmhult is a rural small-town with about 8 000 dwellers residing in the town centre. In the municipality as a whole, there are some 15 500 inhabitants. However, as the municipality homepage is eager to point out, 'Älmhult is not like any other small-town in southern Sweden. Here, the atmosphere is one of a mixture between different influences and values from foreign cultures. Many people from different parts of Sweden and the world work here and the community is continuously visited by people from all over the world' (www.almhult.se, accessed on 21 October 2003). Indeed, there would seem to be good grounds for this assertion, since Älmhult is the cradle of the globally well-known furniture store, IKEA. Älmhult is thus certainly not like any other small-town, especially since it still constitutes the hub in the wheel of IKEA's worldwide retailing suppliers. However, from the events that took place in Älmhult during the year of 2002, it seems as if there were certain limits to the open-mindedness and flexibility that was implied by the municipality's homepage.

In late October 2002, a feature article on the local news pages devoted to Älmhult recounted the bizarre tale of a young woman who had apparently suddenly developed blisters around her mouth after having eaten a pizza from a local pizzeria. There was a quick diagnosis to the effect that she had contracted herpes. The leftovers of the pizza, it was reported, were then promptly taken to the hospital in Ljungby where they had been thoroughly tested. The analysis had showed there to be traces of sperm on the pizza, which accounted for the contagion of herpes (*Smålänningen* 31 October 2002, p. 25). Despite the fact that, even in the headline of the article, it was made clear that the story amounted to a rumour and was not a confirmed event, the whole article still seemed to convey a feeling of 'where there is smoke, there is fire'.

Even though the piece explicitly stated that it was a rumour, however persistent, it is still somewhat surprising that it was published in the first place. Indeed, the news editor of *Smålänningen* admitted to me the dismay he felt when he, while on holiday, picked up the paper at his breakfast table and read the story. In his view, it should never have been printed. However, in an attempt to account for the fact that the article had nonetheless slipped through the net, the editors pointed out that time was often scarce in the printing process and that the control that the central editorial board wielded over articles written at the branch offices was at times less than optimal. This was especially the case regarding articles that were delivered late (interview Davidsson & Gustafsson). In this case, there may well have been a glitch in the internal routines employed by *Smålänningen* on that particular day, and their self-criticism was well justified. The chief focus of our attention, however, is on the societal context that initially bred the rumour.

In the original article, the information officer at the hospital in Ljungby had immediately tried to kill the rumour, pointing out that no such tests had ever been performed on the hospital's premises. Furthermore, he regarded it as highly improbable that any contagious substances found in sperm would stand a chance of surviving the heat inside a pizza oven. However, a civil servant at the municipal Office of Environment and Health played a more ambiguous role when it came to dispelling the rumour. She said that while, on the surface, the story seemed highly improbable, it might well contain 'a grain of truth'. Her rationale for making this assessment was that 'the story had been circulating for quite some time' and that it seemed to retain its basic features every time it resurfaced (*Smålänningen* 31 October 2002, p. 25). In other words, what she chose to treat as factors that indicated the basic accuracy of the story, actually amounted to little more than the most familiar defining characteristics of an urban legend— namely persistence in both frequency and content. And an urban legend is of course precisely what it was.

On sensing their mistake in printing the original article, the newspaper editors were quick to publish rejoinders that might serve to redress the initial impact. Indeed, there was another article on the subject already the very next day. The head medical officer in Älmhult had reacted immediately and forcefully to the article conveying the rumour, and he was now given the floor. The rumour was so stupid, he claimed, that he would rather not make any comments about it, but it was quite clear to him that it was merely an urban legend, a 'Klintberg story'. What was worse, he went on to argue, was that the rumour itself seemed to testify to underlying sentiments of xenophobia in Älmhult (*Smålänningen* 1 November 2002, p. 13).

In completing what must be perceived as a full and complete repentance about the story, *Smålänningen* published another article on the matter a couple of days later, signed by the very journalist who had written the first two pieces. Now, it seemed, munition had been provided that should have been enough to kill the rumour once and for all. To this end, the ethnologist Bengt af Klintberg himself had been brought in to comment on the affair. His verdict was crystal clear; this was an urban legend that was well known to him and it had been in circulation for at least 10-15 years. He had even written about it himself in the second of his two collections of urban legends (Klintberg 1994). It had, on previous occasions, circulated in different communities in southern and central parts of Sweden. This time, it had surfaced in Älmhult with depressing results for two of the local pizzerias, which had been forced to issue public statements, insisting that they had been falsely accused by the rumour and that the infamous pizza had at least not been served on their premises. Klintberg agreed with the municipal head medical officer that the story comprised a sign of budding xenophobia. 'The urban legends are all about our fears of the strange' he said. 'One cannot say that all of them are completely untrue, but they often straddle the borderline between fact and fiction. But the really interesting thing is what the story tells us about Sweden, our fears, and our way of perceiving the world.' (*Smålänningen* 4 November 2002).

Trouble on National Television

So, what does this story tell us? In order to put it into context, we have to deal with another episode involving a pizzeria in Älmhult. Indeed, the aforementioned doctor had already remarked on the connection between the two events in his statement (*Smålänningen* 1 November 2002), and they certainly seemed to be outgrowths of the same basic phenomenon.

On this second occasion, the local newspaper had not been instrumental in spreading the rumour; instead it was quite active in trying to dismantle it. There was, however, another media culprit this time, namely a national investigative TV show by the name of Fläsk (the literal translation of this is 'lard', but since the noun also connotes the expressions 'heavy stuff', 'empty promises' and 'pompous bragging', the term is not directly translatable into English). The TV show in question had recorded the events of an ordinary Saturday night among youths in Älmhult. The reporters had literally dangled the microphone under the noses of drunken youngsters, who had been telling each other stories at the local dance parlour, 'the Silver Valley'. The story on this night had been about the local pizzeria 'Sorello' which, according to the young people interviewed, was suspect in many ways. Accusations were aired to the effect that the pizzeria owners dealt with drugs, that they abused juvenile girls, and that there were rooms for pornographic activities in the basement of the building (*Smålänningen* 3 September 2002, p. 11).

This time, *Smålänningen* reacted promptly and in accordance with press ethical codes in order to stifle the rumours. The newspaper immediately gave the pizzeria owner an opportunity to express his feelings about the media abuse that he had been subjected to. He complained that the TV show had not given him the chance to refute the accusations. Frustration was also evident among the local youth who had appeared in the show, since they believed that they had been maltreated. One of them, the one who had been most visibly drunk, had on the day after the interview tried to withdraw his statement, but had been denied the possibility to do so, on the grounds that what was on record was on record. The teenagers had ostensibly been given false pretexts for the interviews and had thus been tricked into participating in the programme. According to the producers, the original intention had been to expose prevalent tensions between the local majority population and immigrants in a Swedish rural small-town community the size of Älmhult. In this, they had apparently succeeded. The pizzeria owner was very clear in his judgement about the programme: 'All the positive things [we] were discussing, the fact that we enjoy it here in Älmhult, that we have Swedish friends who come here after work to have a cup of coffee, that we have received letters from the municipality thanking us for receiving so many trainees, all these things were left out. They have distorted the truth. . . . I have moved back here twice and I love Älmhult. They wanted to create headlines; to create a negative bomb which they could drop on us and Älmhult' (*Smålänningen* 3 September 2002, p. 11).

A similar view was expressed by a local salesman, who claimed that the producers, in pursuing their own agenda, had tried to convey a nation-wide image of Älmhult as a 'god-forsaken racist stronghold, where people respond in a Texan fashion just because someone drives around in a BMW'. If anyone was serious-minded and well integrated, he concluded, it was the pizzeria owners and he found it to be deeply upsetting that they had not been given a chance to dispute the accusations in the TV show (*Smålänningen* 3 September 2002, p. 11). The producers remained adamant, however. They reiterated that they had wanted to disclose prevalent prejudice about foreigners in a Swedish small-town community. It had, they stated, never been their intention to accuse the pizzeria owner of anything. Remarkably however, they then went on to criticise the pizzeria owner for seeming to believe that the programme could be used as a free commercial and that he could use the opportunity to demonstrate their tasty food and how hard he and his employees worked. That, they stated, had never been the idea. The producer finally also disagreed with the criticism that they had interviewed drunken youngsters: 'Only one out of the five was drunk', she said (*Smålänningen* 3 September 2002, p. 11).

The Incidents Compared

These two cases are instructive in many ways and display interesting similarities, as well as equally noteworthy differences. To first address the similarities, they both in a clear-cut and also disturbing manner convey how images of foreigners and strangers often are deeply gendered.[1] In both cases, a story is told about the unbridled sexuality of immigrant men and the subsequent defilement of young Swedish women, supposedly carried out by these foreigners who reside in the very midst of Swedish society. In the first tale, the adulteration is carried out using a pizza contaminated with herpes, in the second version, young women are drugged and subsequently sexually abused in the basement of the pizza parlour. The underlying morality of the two stories seems to be that the Swedish nation should beware, lest its women be defiled and its people unwittingly corrupted through the very food they are eating. The bodily integrity of the young women is thus considered to be violated, while there is simultaneously also a violation of the symbolic body of the nation to which they belong (Lupton 1999:3, cf. Douglas 1985:80). As aptly put by Eva Mackey (1999:113): 'In modern western cultures, bodies, like individuals and like nations, ideally have firm boundaries between inside and outside, are self-contained and self-regulating, are unified and whole in and of themselves, and do not allow uncontrolled penetration of body boundaries, either by other bodies or substances.' In the two cases mentioned above, such violations were claimed to have occurred and the alarm was thus sounded among the concerned public. The implied message seemed to be that the decent folks needed to make their voices heard in order to stave off the perceived threats emanating from the strangers residing in their community.

There is also an apparent ambiguity at work here, however. Immigrants, widely defined, have in Sweden become an ordinary and almost taken-for-granted component of everyday life, but herein also lies the very danger as conveyed by the story-tellers. Since immigrants are so frequently involved in the fast food business and in restaurant activities, there is perceived to be a major danger lurking in Swedish society. Most of the time, we do not reflect very much about our daily intake of food; eating is in fact one of the most mundane of all conceivable activities. The implied message here however is that the majority We should pause and think about the premises of this everyday routine—before it is too late.

Thus, unwittingly or not, the two stories relay a perceived risk that strangers in our midst steal into our very lives and slowly but steadily transform the country of Sweden, along with its inhabitants. The Swedish nation will purportedly lose its virginity in the process, and the uncontrolled sexual behaviour of male immigrants will have its way in the end. Moreover, it is the nation's women who are clearly depicted as being the weakest link. For it is precisely here that the chain holding the hitherto familiar Swedish society together is likely to burst, unless something is done to rectify the situation. Any such recommendations are not made explicit but, then again, they probably do not need to be. All that is required, according to the implied message, is swift, staunch and manly action, to prevent the scenario from coming true. It is left to the listener to figure out what kind of action this may entail.

As already noted, the actual passing on of the rumours about the vile and immoral activities of the pizzeria owners permits the re-tellers to convey racist sentiments without actively posing as racists themselves; conveniently, they just pass on what they have heard from other, ostensibly reliable sources. And this is certainly one way to locate disturbing strands of prejudice to somewhere outside the Self.

There were also, however, clear and noticeable contrasts between the two reported cases. Identity construction is a context-bound and dynamic process which, in a local community, is no doubt impinged upon by influential local news media. The differences are therefore quite striking between the respective roles that *Smålänningen* played in the two cases involving the rumours about pizzerias in Älmhult. In the case of the urban legend about the infected pizza, we can see that it was chiefly the point when the story was published by the paper that created the acute phase of the affair. In the second case, the paper instead made it possible for the pizzeria owner and others to step forward and refute the story. And whereas the first example conveyed the message about marginalised immigrant others, the second story, at least in its winding-up phase, ushered in impressions that the local inhabitants, regardless of their ethnicity, closed ranks against the perceived wrongdoings committed to them by the TV crew from the faraway capital. Quite clearly, in the second case, Stockholm served as a negative Other and a local united front was formed to defend the interests of the local community in the face of onslaught from the big city.

This local unification was given its symbolic manifestation a few days after the printing of the original story about the second pizzeria. Centrally located in the paper was a photo of a meeting between the pizzeria owner and the young boy whose drunken ramblings had been most outspokenly negative towards the pizzeria. He had now come to apologise to the pizzeria owner and the snapshot showed the two shaking hands. The teenager assured the owner that he had been devastated by the course of events. His family had suffered and he reiterated that he, without success, had tried to revoke his statements from the TV programme. The pizzeria owner emphasised that he had no problem forgiving the boy and stressed that he thought it admirable that he had mustered the strength to come and apologise in person. There were no winners in this story, he argued, only losers (*Smålänningen* 5 September 2002, p. 14).

Acting upon recommendation by the Swedish Press Ombudsman (*Smålänningen* 5 September, p. 14), three local actors affected by the TV programme later decided to file a complaint to the Swedish Broadcasting Commission.[2] They requested an assessment as to whether the standards of the TV show were compatible with the general demands made of public television regarding objectivity, impartiality and the respect for the sanctity of individual citizens' private lives. After some initial deliberations, the complainants did not send a joint statement, but they acted in concert in the sense that they filed their requests simultaneously. In total, complaints were sent by the pizzeria owner, the repentant boy who had apologised to the owner and, finally, by the mother of a

15-year old girl who, in spite of her young age, had also been interviewed in the programme (*Smålänningen* 8 October 2002, p. 11). The concerned mother also happened to be a local politician, who ran for the office of the municipal commissioner in the elections of September 2002. This contributed to the symbolic impact of the action. For, in some sense, the whole small-town community of Älmhult felt itself to have been put on trial by the TV show. Its reputation was at stake and concerted action was needed to ward off the impression that the community was a racist backwater.

Indeed, the paradoxical effect of the screening of the local youth lashing out against the pizzeria seemed to be a welding together of the local population, regardless of whether they were born and bred in the area since many generations back or whether they were immigrants. In this case, the bizarre rumour had been promptly denied, to which end the local newspaper thus played no small part. Otherwise, it is well known that imaginative rumours can have far-reaching consequences for community action. In his seminal study on the anatomy of a rumour that spread through the French city of Orléans, Edgar Morin (1971) recounted fantastical stories about young women who were drugged in the fitting rooms of Jewish-owned fashion boutiques, smuggled through secret tunnels and subsequently sold into networks of prostitution and white slavery in North Africa. As a result of the rumour, concerned citizens organised consumer boycotts against the shops implicated in the story and set up pickets outside their premises. The authorities were so alarmed by the events that they had to organise public meetings and issue official denunciations of the rumour (Dingwall 2001:185). Indeed, there are several points of convergence between the rumour in Orléans and the one in Älmhult; both depict perceived foreigners as the offenders, both are about criminal activities and sexual abuse of young women taking place in subterranean quarters. There is no way of telling in advance what directions the rumours will take, and the Orléans rumour was only a shade more fanciful than Älmhult's counterpart. This is why the remedial actions of the local newspaper were so important. For, as we have seen concerning the story about the infected pizza, where *Smålänningen's* role was decidedly more ambiguous, it was the owners of the two accused pizzerias themselves who had to issue statements insisting that the unfortunate woman had at least not ordered her pizza in their restaurant. They were thus forced to act in a manner which, in effect, only served to confirm the basic truth of the absurd story.

A Third Story and What It Tells Us

And so, despite the fact that pizzerias long ago ceased to be perceived as strange by the broadest strata of Swedish rural settings, it seems as if they are still occasionally seen as the abode of strangers. And strangers constitute an existential challenge and at times even an implicit threat. Hence, this is a plausible breeding ground for such accusations about criminality, sexual abuse and faulty hygiene as were spread by the two stories recounted here. Here it seems as if the pizzeria owner in the story centring on the TV programme ended up being recognised as a confirmed member of the local team, as 'one of ours'. But as already stated, there is no way of telling the outcome in advance.

Indeed, seen through the prism of another news story which played itself out towards the end of the year, there seemed to be something about the combination of pizzerias and Älmhult which suggested a tension that somehow remained unsolved. This time, the police had caught three burglars red-handed, who were transporting loot from a pizzeria in Älmhult in their car. A neighbour had noticed suspicious activities around the pizzeria and had therefore alerted the police, who subsequently found equipment for making kebabs and pizza salad, as well as a robust 20-kilogramme cheese, when they searched the car. The police finally solved the case by matching the shoes of the men in the car to footprints found inside the pizzeria. It was pointed out in the news item that the perpetrators were asylum-seekers temporarily residing at reception facilities in an adjacent municipality (*Smålänningen*, 5 November 2002, p. 11; 21 November 2002, p. 26).

So, why is this incident interesting? It is not about rumours and urban legends, so why retell the story here? Well, the point is that it *is* another case of a stereotyped news report about asylum-seekers and at the same time it also seems to confirm the notion that pizzerias tend to be epitomised as harbourers of the strange. The burglars are depicted as amateurish and not overly clever, while the detailed description of the loot found in their car contributes to giving the story a ridiculous touch. The image of large footprints made in flour and tomato sauce on the pizzeria floor certainly invites amused smiles and sniggers about clumsy would-be perpetrators from a nearby reception centre for asylum-seekers. Why, one may wonder, is the reader told about the kebab-making equipment and the 20-kilogramme cheese? And, even though the pizzeria itself is only the passive crime scene, the ridiculing note and the touch of petty criminality seem to rub off on it as well. There is some form of guilt-by-association at work here, along the lines of implied common knowledge that everyone who works in this line of business is involved in shadowy activities anyway. The contrast becomes especially striking when one notes that the courageous neighbour who alerted the police, and was subsequently awarded a medal by the police for his actions, had a name with a very old and 'Swedish-sounding' ring to it—'Arnold Bengtsson' (*Smålänningen*, 5 November 2002, p. 11; 21 November, p. 26). Here is a sturdy representative of old-fashioned Swedish values, appearing in as great a contrast to the inept burglars as could possibly be imagined. The bottom line, however, is that pizzerias still seem to be seen as the locations of strangers in the local community of Älmhult, and the depictions of them provided by the local newspaper most often do not help to change this. It would appear that there is quite some way to go before the proud descriptions of a state of multicultural peace and harmony on the municipality's homepage match the everyday realities encountered in the community itself.

Concluding the Case: Telling Episodes

At first glance, the differences between the Älmhult episodes and the other cases of story-telling recounted in this book may seem vast. Since the pizzeria stories are so episodic in character, they cannot, for example, be compared to the more persistent themes that frequently recurred in the daily newspaper reporting on local goings-on in Markaryd and Ljungby. For although they certainly comprise a most bizarre plot, they only provide us very quick snapshots of events.

Nonetheless, even though the pizzeria stories constitute a case apart from the more comprehensive narratives studied in the other two cases, they could also be argued to represent a paradigmatic case of how perceived strangers are depicted as being risky to community values. For while, on the surface, the local pizzeria owners seemed to be well integrated and part of the everyday life of the community, they were still being regarded in prevalent discourses as strange, foreign and risky. There was, once again, the underlying, uncompromising sub-division of the population into 'Swedes' and 'foreigners'. Once considered a 'foreigner', there is, according to this rigid worldview, no way of crossing the straits to the other category. Apparently, following popular wisdom, one cannot belong to both categories simultaneously and if one is branded a 'foreigner', one is stuck with that categorisation. Once a 'foreigner', always a 'foreigner'. And, as a 'foreigner', one belongs to a collectivity which, at least tacitly, is claimed to pose a threat to decent local folks, not least their young women. The strangers are held to bring, if not mayhem, then at the very least infectious diseases, un-bridled sexuality, uncleanliness and filth in their wake.

Since it shares the anatomy of a rumour, trying to pinpoint the actual development of an urban legend, once it has been re-hatched, re-constructed and adjusted to local circumstances, is almost impossible. But it can at least be said to be highly context-dependent. In good-weather conditions, there are probably fair prospects to dispel the rumour, so that it does not do further damage to integral bonds between the settled majority and resident minorities. In bad-weather conditions, however, where local discontent is already high because the economic situation is difficult for example, easy answers and their corresponding solutions can easily gain currency. This is when the process of identifying scapegoats is menacingly close at hand and the vulnerable group of relatively newly arrived immigrants makes easy prey. In such cases, the bizarre often becomes the scary and stories with an amusing twist can literally become deadly serious. Indeed, the step from Älmhult to Tsaritsyno need not be so great after all.

Notes

1. I am here indebted to Katharine Tyler and Inbal E. Cicurel, for the valuable comments they have made on this important point.
2. The programme was subsequently freed by the Commission.

8. Lessons and Reflection

In the preceding pages and chapters, I have retold and interpreted stories about strangers from three small-town milieus which happened to be situated in Sweden. This retelling has, in turn, comprised my own story about the stories that were told and thus represents the way that I have interpreted them. I have been guided in this by theoretical perspectives and insights from several literatures, most prominently those focusing on perceptions of socio-cultural risk; stereotype-formation, scapegoating and enemy images; media reporting on immigrants; and the importance of the mundane. In view of the deep and thorough-going fascination that human beings typically have with strangers and their perceived deviations, as well as the challenges that they are considered to bring to deep-seated norms and values, it is no great surprise that these themes have already been extensively dealt with in previous research. It therefore behoves me to ask myself what theoretical contributions I, as a single author, can make to such perennial debates. In view of this, let me thus start this concluding chapter with an outline of what I consider to be my main theoretical input.

Bringing Together Insights

My primary theoretical ambition with this book has not been to open up new and virginal grounds of theory-building. Rather, I have endeavoured to enhance the understanding of the complex reality of majority-minority relations by bringing together several strands of related research in a way that, rather surprisingly given that they are all so closely affiliated, has rarely been done before. Indeed, political science is an academic sub-discipline which is well-known for its propensity to pick up — some would say steal or pinch — concepts, themes and perspectives from adjacent disciplines and so, being a political scientist, this way of proceeding comes fairly naturally to me. Moreover, I believe that this combination of perspectives gives added value to the understanding of majority-minority relations in contemporary Western societies. Let me point out the most central reasons why this is so.

First of all, the combination of insights from the literature on socio-cultural risk with arguments about stereotype-formation adds to the understanding of the rigid and uncompromising nature of beliefs held by resident majorities about immigrated groups. When perceptions about deviations from societal norms are frozen into images connoting risk and latent danger or, worse than that, imminent danger to cherished values, life or property, little room is left for compromise. These dynamics can of course work both ways, giving ample ground for confrontation and resentment both among majorities *and* minorities.

Secondly, the combination of these two fields—socio-cultural risk and stereotype-formation—with the tradition of research into mundane, everyday matters is also fruitful in several respects. Most importantly, it equips the analyst with better tools with which to understand the evident tyranny of everyday life, as it is exercised on marginalised categories of people. For when these persons are deemed to be latently risky and hazardous in ways that hardly allow for change, they do not have much of an opportunity to carve out an everyday existence in their new host societies that can possibly be satisfactory for them as individuals. The negative stereotypes that are held by the silent majority, the decent folks, have a staggering impact. They serve to exclude the strangers from taking part in the everyday, and they reinforce the boundaries constructed by the we-community, held together by common premises of banal localism, nationalism or whatever type of belonging, on whatever scale, that might be relevant 'out there'.

Thirdly, the combination of theorising on socio-cultural risk with the fields of stereotyping and mass media research is valuable for studies into the complex and fateful dynamics that occur when a risk discourse transforms into one of threat and imminent danger. This can most often be found in and, indeed, is frequently partly brought about by, the mass media. Societal developments in such cases clearly leave the mundane and the banal behind. Instead, the course is set for heated encounters and conflict, as well as for individual and collective action believed to be preventative. And as discourses on risk mutate into ones of threat and imminent danger, there is often also a simultaneous metamorphosis from general, frequently exoticising stereotyped perceptions of strangers as latent risk-bearers, into frozen images of enemies who need to be fought or got rid of, or of scapegoats who need to be sacrificed in order for the host society to recover and prosper. The dynamics of such chains of events can be better understood, and hopefully sometimes prevented, through careful analyses of the phenomena involved. I hope that this book can serve to inspire such insights and even work as part of a roadmap to reach such highly desirable goals.

Universal Stereotypes, Everyday Libel

Tendencies to stereotype strangers in such negative ways as those recounted in the chapters above have a sadly universal quality. I would again venture to suggest that examples such as these can be found anywhere in the Western world, and indeed, worldwide. Newcomers and immigrants are deemed to be risky because they are perceived not to fit in. The phenomenon of perceptions of socio-cultural risk is highly nebulous, which is a crucial part of the problem; there is always some undefined, latent fear that needs to be countered, some indeterminate sense that immigrants are deviators from norms that may not, as such, be much reflected on in daily life, but that, due to their relation to perceived traditions, are deemed venerable and precious all the same.

The categories of people that are marginalised and treated as strangers shift across space and time, but the tendency to categorise, marginalise and exclude others seems almost to be inherent to human nature. This may bring hope to certain groups that are currently depicted as strangers and risk-bearers, since their situation could change for the better, if only given time. But what is discomforting is that, generally speaking, there seems to be no way out. Some groups will always be regarded as Other and squeezed out towards the margins of our societies.

In this book I have studied, mainly through the local press, the dynamics of marginalisation in small-town communities in southern Sweden. Several points of departure were inspired by Mary Douglas and her argument that ideas about purity and contamination serve as cornerstones of identity constructions and the exclusion of Others among majority populations, also in contemporary societies in the Western world. This line of thought provides essential and significant insights and there are numerous illustrations of its practicability within these pages. Aside from the purity vs. filth distinction, there are several other related dichotomies at work here: the normal vs. the abnormal, the honest vs. the criminal, the hardworking vs. the welfare recipient etc. What they share is that they are all based on the same fundamental premises. Their common denominator is that the social world can be sub-divided into the category of Us, who represent normality, and Them, who stand for an abnormality that is always somehow threatening.

The reader may further recall that Douglas discerned three structures of libel in discourse about foreigners. The mildest variant, the food libel, implies that foreigners eat disgusting foods; the sex libel is the accusation that they represent menacingly uncontrolled sexuality and that they are prone to defile our women or else take them away from us; and, finally, the most serious one, the blood libel, according to which the enemy is already here and s/he is out to inflict bodily harm on us, maybe even to take our very lives. The trichotomy is thought-provoking but it did not in all respects match the Swedish settings that I studied. The sex libel was definitely present, both in terms of the fanciful urban legends about the pizzerias in Älmhult and in the reports about rapes committed by inmates at the asylum-seeker compound in Markaryd (where it, in contrast with other cases, was explicitly pointed out that the perpetrator was of foreign origin).

Even so, matters did not get so much out of hand that it was justified to talk about a blood libel in action; instead, it was reportedly property rather than lives that was being put at risk through the designs of certain categories of immigrants. Thieving and burglaries were, according to the analysed discourses, held to be frequent felonies among immigrants and strangers. Moreover, according to one prevalent strand of discourse, the immigrants who were seen to be a burden—and that seemed to be a vast category—also constituted a risk, if not to life and property, then to the economy. The food libel was not discernible in the local settings of the study, however, as the sharing of food actually seemed to form one of the first inroads into inviting minority groups to have some rudimentary contact with the majority. This then was a ray of hope, although it is questionable how the openness to tasting food from foreign countries could really aid the integration of minority groups. For it indicates a process of exoticising at work and it certainly does not invite the immigrants into the everyday.

Damned if They Do and Damned If They Don't—But Still

Writers that promote ideas of increasing diversity are sometimes accused of being overly demanding in their assessments of, for example, state or municipal action, or media coverage of immigrant issues. For, on the one hand, if nothing is said on the matter, by either the politicians or the media, it is often argued that the problem is being glossed over or ignored, which, of course, is believed to be bad. If, on the other hand, the media and politicians criticise liberal immigration policies and demand greater levels of restrictiveness regarding, for instance, the reception of asylum-seekers, this is branded as even worse. Conversely, if well-intended integration programmes are established, if benefits are doled out, and if the media writes about this accordingly, the criticism is that all of this amounts to charity, to do-gooder mentality and to efforts by the host community to feel good about itself. Those who do good deeds may be caring but are still regarded as paternalistic, over-protective and somehow suspect. In other words, the authorities and the media alike are damned if they do and damned if they don't.

There is some truth to this criticism, and I believe that I too, along with many other writers on the subject, have at times been on the erring side, too eager to find something to criticise in the prevailing discourses and practices under study. When this happens, it is a case of empathising and sympathising with the underdog, no matter what. I would still argue, however, that there *are* some tendencies in even the most well-intended exercises at promoting majority-minority understanding that really should be criticised. Most typically, some of the episodes recounted in the chapters above have shown that, when the society of the majority community tried to promote inter-group understanding, this was often done by inviting representatives of minority groups to sing something nice, dance an exotic dance or prepare some exciting 'ethnic' food. The potential enemy image might well be dissolved after such exercises, at least momentarily, which is no doubt positive, but does it really help these groups to successfully integrate into the everyday lives of the host community? As already stated, the answer here is clearly no. The dichotomisation of majority and minority is cemented even further, and the status of the latter group as marginalised strangers is accentuated. For while majority groups may be inclined to accept exotic strangers when they arrive in insignificant numbers, should larger groups emerge, a risk discourse may very well evolve regarding precisely this exotic, or unchained quality, which all of a sudden is seen to pose a latent danger to more familiar and ingrained ways of being.

Is There Anything We Can Do?

So, what should we do? Resign ourselves to the idea that the uncompromising subdivision between Us and Them is an endemic human condition and then do nothing further about it? Perhaps one need not be that rash. History has shown that there are different ways in which the status as a marginalised stranger is materialised, some better and some worse. In most Western settings there have been changes for the better with the passing of the centuries. After all, unlike in the Middle Ages, suspected witches are no longer burnt at the stakes in Europe. In other respects our contemporary times can seem to be less enlightened and equally repressive, even if these new forms of repression are most of the time more subtle than those practiced in the Dark Ages.

Either way, few would deny that a less prolific employment of outright enemy images would benefit both majorities and minority groups. This is a development which is not easy to bring about, not least considering the situation prompted by September 11, 2001, after which a blanket demonisation of Muslims has taken place in several Western media, as well as in other fora of public discourse. A frequent overuse of enemy images is no doubt detrimental to societal life at large. A climate of widespread suspicion is to nobody's gain; rather it tends to become paralysing in several respects. This is of course not to deny that there are real dangers out there. There is doubtless a terrorist threat against Western lives and values emanating from extremist quarters, but the 'war on terror' and its accompanying distrustful and suspicious discourses have grown way out of proportion.

To my mind, the most treacherous of the stereotype structures discussed above are the scapegoat imagery. For not only are the scapegoats alleged to be enemies, or even *the only* detectable enemies, but, because of their vulnerability, they are also easy to attack, physically as well as verbally. Indeed, scapegoat-prone thinking seems to trigger the most primitive instincts about corrective and preventive action. Above, I have made some references to the extreme case of the Russian-Chechen war, but it is unnerving to note that essentially the same underlying dynamics of scapegoat-formation could be discerned in the low-level but almost community-wide outbursts against asylum-seekers that took place in Markaryd. As burglaries and thefts in the area increased, economic indicators slumped and the general appeal of the municipality decreased, the community

began to ask itself who was to blame. And there was a ready answer: the asylum-seekers of course! Even in view of countervailing evidence and the knowledge that these were largely unsubstantiated claims, the solution seemed to be so
patently clear. The general view seemed to be that, if only the asylum-seekers
were relocated elsewhere, all other problems in the community would be solved.

But, again, where do we even begin to change all this? Is there no way of
getting around these categorical, dichotomous structures of talk and thought?
Well, first of all, to use Michael Billig's familiar expression, the banal -isms of
nationalism, localism, racism, etc., must be recognised to be the mothers of all
hot, uncompromising and conflict-seeking '-isms'. The many ways in which the
marking of distances between the majority and the group of perceived strangers
are continuously made on an everyday basis form the preconditions for the justi-
fication of subsequent, aggressive actions in conflict-ridden situations. Open
xenophobia, jingoism and racism would not be so relentless sentiments if they
were not built up and maintained on a continual basis, on seemingly innocent
grounds. Once the genie has slipped out of the bottle in a conflict, once a discourse of imminent threat has escalated and left the more vague risk discourse
behind, it is too late to take remedial action. And, so, one needs to start with the
little things. For it is not the barren land that gives the crop a good potential to
grow.

Clearly, this is where educational institutions at different levels of society
have to get to work. Curricula and textbooks must not permit the unreflected reinforcement of stereotypes about immigrants and perceived strangers. These
texts cannot be checked through carefully or often enough. This is not necessarily a call for political correctness and it is certainly not a call for censorship. It
is, however, a call for a heightened awareness that it is precisely the little things
that *do* matter, and that what might seem to be innocuous details can in fact signal the approval of rigid demarcation lines between the majority and minorities
in a society.

Equally clearly, both the local and national media have a key role to play in
any attempt to counteract the stranglehold of established stereotypes. Remem-
bering that the media—like all institutions—are a constituent part of society,
they are of course party to trends that characterise that society in general. They
do not live a life of their own and thus cannot free themselves completely from
the ingrained structures of thought that condition actions in the surrounding
community. There are therefore limits to what they can reasonably do. Even so,
the media also play the role of an actor in their own right, and they certainly
constitute an elite group within society. They thus have a certain responsibility
to lead the way, together with prominent and responsible politicians, intellectu-
als and other key groups within the community.

Nonetheless, the media seldom construct stereotypes from a clean slate, but
rather reinforce stereotypical images that are somehow already prevalent in public discourse. What is needed, I believe, is once again a heightened awareness of
how seemingly innocent remarks can be read as condemning and stigmatising.
As shown above, one typical example of this comprises those stories that, on the
surface, appear to recount the success of those individual immigrants who have

made it, often against all conceivable odds, but where the subtext clearly implies instead that these are but the exceptions that prove the rule. According to this logic, the bulk of the other immigrants are either seen to be criminal elements or burdensome welfare-recipients, or indeed both of these. Awareness about the importance of such subtle indices can be brought about, partly at least, by internal education and an active dialogue with the surrounding society, not least with the immigrants themselves.

In raising awareness of the devious mechanisms of the self-perpetuating '—isms', it is important to note that well-intended euphemisms often do not make things better. I recently had a discussion with a student who, on good grounds, believed that referring to troubled urban areas as being 'densely populated by immigrants' was quite likely to breed stereotypical images about crime-prone strangers among the majority. She quoted an expert who instead favoured the term 'sparsely populated by Swedes'. I however strongly disagreed with the expert's wording; the suggested formula would only make matters worse. The negative, finger-pointing effect would remain, on top of which, one would also, despite all well-meaning intention, indicate that an 'immigrant' could never become 'a Swede'. And so, the underlying dichotomisation would only be reinforced.

From Risk to Threat Discourse

So, what circumstances can we identify as being instrumental for the development of a risk discourse into one of threat and imminent danger? It is, as always, hard to draw any general and definite conclusions, but, inspired by the cases analysed in the preceding chapters, there are definitely some points that should be made. First of all and most obviously, the dynamics of such developments are context-bound. If general causes of discontent abound on a community level, it is a temptingly quick and easy solution to seek scapegoats. If the economy is weak, if unemployment rates go up, if the weather is grey—the reasons are manifold and various.

Secondly, there is the factor of irresponsible actors at different levels of society who pave the way for escalations into discourses of threat and imminent danger. One can, for example, conceive of the vote-maximising politician who cannot resist the temptation to turn the issue of locally received asylum-seekers into a trump card in local electioneering. Striving to appeal to a broad spectrum of voters, s/he exploits local discontent and suspicion and so targets vulnerable groups. One can also envisage the editor or journalist of an influential newspaper or media channel, who chooses to convey rumours incriminating against immigrants despite a lack of proper corroboration. As discussed above, rumours can then easily start to live lives of their own. One also should not forget the individual immigrant perpetrator her-/himself, the one who actually commits criminal acts, despite being aware of the potential sanctions and knowing that s/he might bring the entire group of fellow immigrants/asylum-seekers/refugees into disrepute. Reports about perpetrations by immigrants are certainly not altogether fictitious, exaggerated or made up, so this aspect should of course be kept in mind.

Then, finally, there is an element of incidence, chance or quite simply bad luck. Sometimes it is simply unpredictable when the sparks will ignite, when a rumour depicting wrong-doing and menacing strangers will be believed at face value. In the chapters above, most of the attention has been devoted to normally tranquil small-towns and, as a rule, non-dramatic and peaceful settings. I have repeatedly argued the necessity of studying the everyday, since it is the living conditions in mundane life which, for most people, constitute the most essential part of their existence. In milieus where, most of the time, nothing much out of the ordinary seems to happen, it need not take very large transgressions of local mores and rules to provoke harsh condemnations and uncompromising back-lashes. Again, remember the woman who invited the garbage-collectors in for a nice cup of tea.

The Omnipresent Narratives of Superiority

However desirable it would be to declare that the predominance of nation-states and the salience of national borders are anomalies in the face of globalisation, there is no discernible evidence of any thorough-going changes in these respects within the next generations. In spite of all argument to the contrary, the West-phalian nation-state system has proven itself to be remarkably sturdy and retains most of its influence and dominance in our contemporary world. And as long as the individual members of nation-states are awarded membership status through limited and exclusive citizenships, there will be outsiders and insiders, the latter of whom will guard their positions more or less anxiously.

Equally fundamentally, the iron grip of stereotypes is a question of power. Our identities are constructed in the interface between Self and Other, an enter-prise in which third positions do not seem relevant. The group corresponding to the Self can be re-labelled in several ways; the in-group as opposed to the out-group, the haves as opposed to the have-nots, the superior as opposed to the subordinate, or the privileged as opposed to the marginalised. Repeating my pessimistic view, to break the predominance of dichotomous worldviews hardly seems possible. They are simply too ingrained in the ways that we live, think and act as humans together with and in opposition to others. If we want to rem-edy the situation regarding the relations between settled majorities and migrated minority groups it seems that we are stuck with working with what we have. That basically means settling for achieving increased levels of dialogue and un-derstanding—somehow. To specify in more practical terms what this entails more exactly is no easy matter. Nonetheless, if immigrants are depicted as part of the everyday and treated accordingly in societal texts and talk, then they at least stand a better chance of not being scapegoated. And perhaps then some downright tragic outcomes could be avoided.

In order to be a part of the everyday of the majority society, immigrants need to be able to cross the various straits of that society and be admitted into

positions that, to a depressingly large extent, are the preserve of the majority elites. Only then will these fundamental and conditioning discursive power structures slowly start to erode, especially the ones according to which the majority
represents the normal that, due to its familiarity and taken-for-grantedness, is
invisible, and where the minority position always is the abnormal and highly
visible one. The task is daunting. For centuries the meta-narrative of the superiority of Western civilisation has reigned supreme in the Western world. It is
ever-present among its residents and is in its seemingly innocent and banal
forms reproduced on a daily basis in their lives.

We have here only studied minuscule parts of these structures, namely those
reflected in the public narratives that characterise local media coverage in three
Swedish municipalities. They translate into unfathomably larger structures, in
Sweden and in the West. This is also why finger-pointing in the direction of erring actors in Markaryd, Ljungby and Älmhult is all too easy, but also unfair and
fundamentally pointless. The expressions of banal localism and even racism un-
veiled there do not even represent the tip of an iceberg. These cases might, however, inspire us to start with ourselves. It may be useful to undertake some soul-
searching on an individual basis; who are the Us and who are the Others that I
differentiate between in my daily practices and on what grounds do I separate
between them?

Again, there is thus a need to start with the little things. In order to, collectively, make a difference, we must look into the practices of our own everyday.
The mundane might be banal but it is also all-important. Unless immigrants are
admitted into the everyday course and discourse of community life, they are
prone to remain strangers, and so stories will continue to be told about them. At
worst, these will convey tales about the risky, the dangerous, the threatening and
the unnerving. At best, they will contain descriptions of the bizarre, the colour-
ful and the exotic, but they will never be neutral, and they will continue to sus-
tain the exclusion of strangers from the mainstream life of our societies.

Bibliography

Aftonbladet (2000) 22 October.

Aho, James A. (1994) *This Thing of Darkness. A Sociology of the Enemy.* Seattle: University of Washington Press.

Anderson, Benedict (1983) *Imagined Communities.* London: Verso.

Argounova, Tatiana (2001) *Scapegoats of Natsionalizm: ethnic tensions in Sakha (Yakutia), northeastern Russia,* unpublished Ph.D. Dissertation, Scott Polar Research Institute, University of Cambridge.

Back, Les (1996) *New Ethnicities and Urban Culture: Racism and Multiculture in Young Lives,* London: UCL Press.

Bal, Mieke (1985) *Narratology: Introduction to the theory of narrative.* Toronto: University of Toronto Press.

Bar-Tal, Daniel (2000) *Shared Beliefs in a Society. Social Psychological Analysis.* Thousand Oaks: Sage.

Barany, Zoltan (2002) *The East European Gypsies. Regime Change, Marginality, and Ethnopolitics.* Cambridge: Cambridge University Press.

Barber, Benjamin (1995) *Jihad vs. McWorld.* New York: Ballantine Books.

Bauman, Zygmunt (1998) *Globalization. The Human Consequences,* Cambridge: Polity Press.

Beck, Ulrich (1992) *Risk Society: Towards a New Modernity.* London: Sage,

Berger, Arthur Asa (1997) *Narratives in Popular Culture, Media and Everyday Life.* Thousand Oaks: Sage.

Bhabha, Homi K. (1990) 'DissemiNation: Time, narrative and the margins of the modern nation', Homi K. Bhabha (ed.): *Nation and Narration.* London: Routledge.

Bhabha, Homi K. (1994) *The Location of Culture.* London: Routledge.

Billig, Michael (1995). *Banal Nationalism.* London: Sage.

Billig, Michael et al (1988) *Ideological Dilemmas. A Social Psychology of Everyday Thinking.* London: Sage.

Bishop, Hywel & Adam Jaworski (2003) '"We beat 'em": nationalism and the hegemony of homogeneity in the British press reportage of Germany versus England during Euro 2000', *Discourse & Society* 14:3, 243-272.

Borevi, Karin & Per Strömblad (2004) 'Kategorisering och integration – en introduktion', Karin Borevi & Per Strömblad (eds): *Kategorisering och integration. Om föreställda identiteter i politik, forskning, media och vardag.* Stockholm: SOU 2004:48.

Brekhus, Wayne (2000) 'A Mundane Manifesto', *Journal of Mundane Behavior*, 1:1 http://www.mundanebehavior.org/issues/v1n1/brekhus.htm (accessed 2003-06-11).

Brune, Ylva (2002) '"Invandrare" i mediearkivets typgalleri', Paulina de los Reyes, Irene Molina och Diana Mulinari (eds): *Maktens (o)lika förklädnader.* Stockholm: Atlas.

Brune, Ylva (2004) 'Nyhetslogik och främlingssyn i mediernas konstruktion av 'invandrare', Karin Borevi & Per Strömblad (eds): *Kategorisering och integration. Om föreställda identiteter i politik, forskning, media och vardag.* Stockholm: SOU 2004:48.

Brunvand, Jan Harold (1981) *The Vanishing Hitchhiker: Urban Legends and their Meanings.* New York: Norton.

Brunvand, Jan Harold (1984) *The Choking Doberman and other 'New' Urban Legends.* New York: Norton.

Castells, Manuel (1996) *The Information Age: Economy, Society and Culture.: Vol. I: The Rise of the Network Society.* Malden (Mass.) and Oxford: Blackwell Publishers.

Castles, Stephen & Mark J. Miller (2003) *The Age of Migration. International Population Movements in the Modern World.* Third Edition. Houndmills, Basingstoke: Palgrave Macmillan.

Cohen, Stanley (1985) *Visions of Social Control. Crime, Punishment and Classification.* Cambridge: Polity Press.

Cohen, Stanley (1987) *Folk Devils & Moral Panics. The Creation of Mods and Rockers.* Oxford: Basil Blackwell (3rd ed.).

Dagens Nyheter (2002) 12 June.

Dahlstedt, Magnus (2005) *Reserverad demokrati*. Umeå: Boréa.

Danjoux, Olivier (2002) *L'État, c'est pas moi. Reframing Citizenship(s) in the Baltic Republics*. Lund: Department of Political Science.

DeGroot, Gerard J: (2001) "When Nothing Happened": History, Historians and the Mundane", *Journal of Mundane Behavior* 2:1, http://www.mundanebehavior.org/issues/v2n1.degroot.htm (accessed 2003-06-11).

Dingwall, Robert (2001) 'Contemporary legends, rumours and collective behaviour: some neglected resources for medical sociology?', *Sociology of Health and Illness*, 23: 2, 180-202.

Douglas, Tom (1995) *Scapegoats. Transferring Blame*. London: Routledge.

Douglas, Mary (1985) *Risk Acceptability According to the Social Sciences*. New York: Russell Sage Foundation.

Douglas, Mary (1992): *Risk and Blame: Essays in Cultural Theory*. London: Routledge.

Douglas, Mary (2002) *Purity and Danger: An analysis of concept of pollution and taboo*. London: Routledge.

Ekecrantz & Olsson, Jan & Tom Olsson (1998) *Det redigerade samhället. Om journalistikens, beskrivningsmaktens och det informerade förnuftets historia*. Stockholm: Carlssons.

Elgström, Ole (2000) *Images and Strategies for Autonomy. Explaining Swedish Security Policy Strategies in the 19th Century*. Dordrecht: Kluwer.

Elias, Norbert & John L. Scotson (1999) *Etablerade och outsiders. En sociologisk studie om grannskapsproblem*. Lund: Arkiv.

Ellegård, Kajsa (2001) 'Fånga vardagen – hur och varför?' Kajsa Ellegård & Elin Wihlborg (eds): *Fånga vardagen. Ett tvärvetenskapligt perspektiv*, Lund: Studentlitteratur.

Entman, Robert M. and Andrew Rojecki (2000) *The Black Image in the White Mind. Media and Race in America*. Chicago: Chicago University Press.

Erjavec, Karmen (2003) 'Media construction of identity through moral panics: discourses of immigration in Slovenia', *Journal of Ethnic and Migration Studies*, 29:1, 83-101.

Falkheimer, Jesper (2004) *Att gestalta en region: källornas strategier och mediernas föreställningar om Öresund*. Göteborg: Makadam.

Fennelly, Katherine (2005) 'Latinos, Africans and Asians in the North Star State: Immigrant Communities in Minnesota', Elzbieta M. Gozdziak & Susan F. Martin (eds.): *Beyond the Gateway: Immigrants in a Changing America*. Lanham: Lexington Books.

Fiske, John (1996) *Media matters: race and gender in U.S. politics*. Minneapolis: University of Minnesota Press.

130   Bibliography

Flowerdew John, David C.S. Li and Sarah Tran (2002) "Discriminatory news discourse: some Hong Kong data", *Discourse & Society* 13:3, 319-345.

Foucault, Michel (1991) 'Governmentality', G. Burchell, C. Gordon & P. Miller (eds): *The Foucault Effect: Studies in Governmentality*. Hemel Hampstead: Harvester Wheatsheaf.

Gandy, Oscar H. Jr. & Zhan Li (2005) 'Framing Comparative Risk: A Preliminary Analysis', *the Howard Journal of Communication*, 16:71-86.

Giddens, Anthony (1999) *Runaway World: How Globalisation is Reshaping Our Lives*. London: Profile.

Gilens, Martin (1999) *Why Americans Hate Welfare. Race, Media, and the Politics of Antipoverty Policy*, The University of Chicago Press, Chicago.

Gilroy, Paul (2002) *'There ain't no black in the Union Jack': the cultural politics of race and nation*. London: Routledge.

Grillo, Ralph (2005) "'Saltdean can't Cope": Protests against asylum-seekers in an English seaside suburb', *Ethnic and Racial Studies* 28:2, 235-260.

Guillaumin, Colette (1974): 'Changes in inter-ethnic "attitudes" and the influence of the mass media as shown by research in French-speaking countries', *Race as News*, Paris: Unesco Press.

Haavisto, Camilla (2002) 'Raskrig eller oskyldiga pojkstreck? Diskursanalys av ett urval artiklar om händelserna i Håkansböle hösten 2000', Tom Sandlund (ed.): *Etnicitetsbilden i finlandssvenska medier*. Helsingfors: SSKH Meddelanden Nr. 62.

Haavisto, Camilla (2003) 'Konstruktionen av "vi" och "de" i den finländska massmediediskursen', Annika Forsander & Matti Similä (eds): *Cultural diversity and integration in the Nordic welfare state*. Helsingfors: SSKH Meddelanden Nr. 65.

Hall, Stuart (1997, ed.) *Representation: Cultural Representations and Signifying Practices*. London: Sage.

Harle, Vilho (2000) *The Enemy with a Thousand Faces. The Tradition of the Other in Western Political Thought and History*, Westport, Connecticut: Praeger.

Harris, S. (1997) 'Everyday Architecture', in S. Harris and D. Berke (eds): *Architecture of the Everyday*, New York: Princeton Architectural Press.

Hartmann, Paul; Charles Husband & Jean Clark (1974) 'Race as News. A Study of the handling of race in the British national press from 1963 to 1970', *Race as News*. Paris: The Unesco Press.

Harvey, David (1989) *The condition of postmodernity: an enquiry into the origins of cultural change*. Oxford: Blackwell.

Hedetoft, Ulf (1990) 'Det nationale fremmedbillede som kulturelt tegn eller: Om at sætte forskelle i verden', Gunhild Agger, Barbara Gentikow & Ulf Hedetoft (eds): *Stereotyper i Europa*, Aarhus: Aarhus universitetsforlag.

Hedetoft, Ulf (2003) 'The Politics of Belonging and Migration in Europe: Raisons d'État and the Borders of the National', Bo Petersson & Eric Clark (eds): *Identity Dynamics and the Construction of Boundaries*. Lund: Nordic Academic Press.

Hellström, Anders (2006, forthcoming) *Bringing Europe Down to Earth*. Lund: Department of Political Science.

Hernes, Gudmund (1978) 'Det mediavridde samfunn', Gudmund Hernes (ed): *Forhandlingsoekonomi og blandningsadministrasjon*, Bergen: Universitetsforlaget.

Hier, Sean P. (2003) 'Risk and panic in late modernity: implications of the converging sites of social anxiety', *British Journal of Sociology* 54: 1, 3-20.

Hier, Sean P. & Joshua L. Greenberg (2002) 'Constructing a discursive crisis: risk, problematization and *illegal* Chinese in Canada', *Ethnic and Racial Studies* 25:3, 490-513.

Hinton, Perry R. (1999) *Stereotypes, Social Cognition and Culture*. Hove: Routledge.

Hirshberg, Matthew S. (1993) 'The Self-Perpetuating National Self-Image: Cognitive biases in perceptions of international interventions', *Political Psychology*, 14:1, 77-98.

Hylland Eriksen, Thomas (2001) 'Kulturell urenhet og innvandrerdebatten', *Vetenskapssocieteten i Lund: Årsbok 2001*. Lund: Vetenskapssocieteten.

Hylland Eriksen, Thomas (2004) *Rötter och fötter: Identitet i en föränderlig tid*. Nora: Nya Doxa.

Ivashchenko, Elena (2001) 'Po obe storony pogroma', *Moskovskie novosti*, No. 45, November 6-12, 3.

Jack, Andrew (2004) *Inside Putin's Russia*. London: Granta.

Jarvis, Darry S. L. (2004) 'Review article: The expanding universe of risk', *Contemporary Politics*, 10:3-4, 305-317.

Jessen, Ulrika; Emma Nordenstedt & Sarina Sandman (1999) 'En läsarundersökning om Smålänningens bilaga "med mera"', Göteborg: Göteborgs universitet: Institutionen för Journalistik och Masskommunikation, JMG (unpublished undergraduate student's paper).

Johansson, Bengt (1998) *Nyheter mitt ibland oss. Kommunala nyheter, personlig erfarenhet och lokal opinionsbildning*. Göteborg: Institutionen för journalistik och masskommunikation, Göteborgs universitet.

Kallus, Rachel (2004) 'The Political Role of the Everyday', *City* 8:3, 341-361.

Kearney, Richard (2003) *Strangers, Gods and Monsters: Interpreting Otherness*. London: Routledge.

Kinnvall, Catarina (2004) 'Globalization and Religious Nationalism: Self, Identity and the Search for Ontological Security', *Political Psychology* 25:5, 741-767.

Kisriev, Enver (2004) 'Republic of Dagestan: Nation-building inside Russia's womb', Pål Kolstø & Helge Blakkisrud (eds): *Nation-Building and Common Values in Russia*, Lanham: Rowman & Littlefield.

af Klintberg, Bengt (1990) *Råttan i pizzan. Folksägner i vår tid.* Stockholm: Pan.

af Klintberg, Bengt (1994) *Den stulna njuren : sägner och rykten i vår tid.* Stockholm: Norstedts.

Kratz, Charlotta (1995) 'Storstad och landsort' in Lennart Weibull & Charlotta Kratz (eds): *Tidningsmiljöer. Dagstidningsläsning på 1990-talet.* Göteborg: Institutionen för journalistik och masskommunikation, Göteborgs universitet.

Kristeva, Julia (1991) *Strangers to Ourselves*, New York: Harvester Wheatsheaf.

Kushner, Tony (2003) 'Meaning nothing but good: ethics, history and asylum-seeker phobia in Britain', *Patterns of Prejudice*, 37:3, 257-276.

Larsson, Larsåke (1998) *Nyheter i samspel. Studier i kommunjournalistik,* Göteborg: Institutionen för journalistik och masskommunikation, Göteborgs universitet.

Lindberg, Christer (1998) *Den gode och den onde vilden,* Lund: Arkiv förlag.

Lupton, Deborah (1999) 'Introduction: risk and sociocultural theory', Deborah Lupton (ed.): *Risk and Sociocultural Theory: New Directions and Perspectives*, Cambridge: Cambridge University Press.

Lynn, Nick and Susan Lea (2003) '"A phantom menace and the new Apartheid": the social construction of asylum-seekers in the United Kingdom', *Discourse and Society* 14: 4, 425-452.

Mackey, Eva (1999) 'Constructing an endangered nation: risk, race and rationality in Australia's native title debate', Deborah Lupton (ed.): *Risk and Sociocultural theory: new directions and perspectives.* Cambridge: Cambridge University Press.

May, David (2001) 'Die Etablierten-Aussenseiter-Beziehung als Grammatik urbanen Zusammenlebens', Wolf-Dietrich Bukow, Claudia Nikodem, Erika Schulze & Erol Yildiz (ed.): *Auf dem Weg zur Stadtgesellschaft. Die multikulturelle Stadt zwischen globaler Neuorientierung und Restauration.* Opladen: Leske & Budrich.

McQuail, Denis (2000) *McQuail's Mass Communication Theory*, 4th ed, London: Sage.

Mellema, Gregory (2000) 'Scapegoats', *Criminal Justice Ethics*, Winter/Spring 2000 (ebsco).

Moon, Dreama G. & Thomas K. Nakayama (2005). 'Strategic Social Identities and Judgments: A Murder in Appalachia', *the Howard Journal of Communications* 16, 87-107.

Morin, Edgar (1971) *Ryktet i Orléans*. Stockholm: Pan.

Mörkenstam, Ulf (2004) 'Foreigners, Immigrants, or New Swedes? The Construction of Immigrants in Swedish Politics during the 20th Century'. Paper for the Ninth International Conference of the International Society for the Study of European Ideas (ISSEI), Pamplona, 2-8 August.

Nord, Lars & Gunnar Nygren (2002) *Medieskugga*. Stockholm: Atlas.

Nordahl Svendsen, Erik (1979) *Avisen i lokalsamfundet. Skive Folkeblad og Herning Folkeblad*. Aarhus: Institut for Presseforskning.

Norman, Karin (2004) 'Equality and Exclusion: "Racism" in a Swedish Town', *Ethnos* 69:2, 204-228.

Nygren, Gunnar (2001) *Medier och medborgare i den digitala kommunen. En undersökning om lokal politisk kommunikation i medier och på kommunala webbplatser*. Stockholm: JMK, Stockholms universitet.

Nylund, Mats (2000) 'Att vinkla etnicitet: En preliminär analys av rubriker och roller i nyheter om etniska minoriteter i finlandssvensk dagspress', Tom Sandlund (ed): *Rasism och etnicitet i den finlandssvenska tidningspressen*. Helsingfors: SSKH Meddelanden Nr. 57.

Olsson, Tom (2002) 'The Right to Talk Politics in Swedish Journalism 1925-1995', M. Hurd, T. Olsson and P. Åker (eds): *Storylines. Media, Power and Identity in Modern Europe. Festschrift for Jan Ekecrantz*. Stockholm: Hjalmarsson och Högberg.

Parekh, Bhikhu (2000). *Rethinking Multiculturalism: Cultural diversity and political theory*. Cambridge: Harvard University Press.

Petersson, Bo (1998) 'Russian Self-Images in Perm', Klas Göran Karlsson; Bo Petersson & Barbara Törnquist-Plewa (eds): *Collective Identities in an Era of Transformations. Analysing developments in East and Central Europe and the former Soviet Union*, Lund: Lund University Press.

Petersson, Bo (2001) *National Self-Images and Regional Identities in Russia*, Aldershot: Ashgate.

Petersson, Bo & Alexa Robertson (2003) 'Inledning', Bo Petersson & Alexa Robertson (eds): *Identitetsstudier i praktiken*, Malmö: Liber.

Petersson, Bo & Anders Hellström (2004) 'Stereotyper i vardagen: Bilder av "de främmande"', Karin Borevi and Per Strömblad (eds): *Kategorisering och integration. Om föreställda identiteter i politik, forskning, media och vardag*. Stockholm: SOU 2004:48.

Petersson, Olof & Ingrid Carlberg (1990) *Makten över tanken. En bok om det svenska massmediesamhället*. Stockholm: Carlssons.

Pettersson, Rune (2003) *Rubriker – bruk och missbruk*. Stockholm: Sellin & Partner.

Pietikäinen, Sari (2003) 'Indigenous identity in print: representations of the Sami in news discourse', *Discourse & Society*, 14:5, 581-610.

Pred, Allan (2000) *Even in Sweden: Racisms, Racialized Spaces, and the Popular Geographical Imagination*. Berkeley: University of California Press.

'Projekt 43 – Ljungby mot rasism' (2001). Unpublished position paper, Municipality of Ljungby.

Ray, Larry & Kate Reed (2005) 'Community, mobility and racism in a semi-rural area: Comparing minority experience in East Kent', *Ethnic and Racial Studies* 28:2, 212-234.

Riggins, Stephen Harold (1997) "The Rhetoric of Othering", S.H. Riggins (ed.): *The Language and Politics of Exclusion: Others in Discourse*. Thousand Oaks: Sage.

Robertson, Roland (1992) *Globalization: social theory and global culture*. London: Sage.

Said, Edward (1993) *Orientalism*. Stockholm: Ordfront.

Sandlund, Tom (2002) 'Diversitet och identitet. Medierna som spegel', Tom Sandlund (ed): *Etnicitetsbilden i svenska medier*, SSKH Meddelanden 62, CEREN Helsingfors.

Scholte, Jan Aart (2000) *Globalization. A Critical Introduction*. Houndmills: Palgrave.

Sibley, David (1995) *Geographies of Exclusion. Society and Difference in the West*. London: Routledge.

Sjöberg, Lennart & Elisabeth Engelberg (2005) 'Lifestyles, Risk Perception and Consumer Behavior', *International Review of Sociology*, 15:2, 327-362.

Skive Folkeblad (2002) January 2 – December 31.

Smålänningen (1987) January 2 – December 31.

Smålänningen (2002) January 2 – December 31.

Solomos, John (1998) *Black Youth, Racism and the State*. Cambridge: Cambridge University Press.

Somers, Margaret (1994). 'The narrative construction of identity: a relational and network approach', *Theory and Society* 23:5, 605-49.

Starnawski, Marcin (2003) 'Nationalist discourse and the ultra-conservative press in contemporary Poland: a case study of *Nasz Dziennik*', *Patterns of Prejudice* 37:1, 65-81.

Stripple, Johannes (2005) *Climate Change after the International: Rethinking Security, Territory and Authority*. Lund: Department of Political Science.

Sydsvenska Dagbladet (2002) 7 June.

Taibbi, Matt (2001) 'Pogroms Return to Russia', *Johnson's Russia List*, November 15, http://www.cdi.org/russia/johnson/5546.cfm.

Tajfel, Henri (1982) *Social Identity and Intergroup Relations*. New York: Cambridge University Press.

Tilly, Charles (2002) *Stories, Identities, and Political Change*. Lanham, Maryland: Rowman & Littlefield.

Törnquist-Plewa, Barbara (2000) 'Speglar vi oss i varandra? Några funderingar kring de nationella stereotypernas beskaffenhet', Barbara Törnquist-Plewa (ed.): *Sverige och Polen: nationer och stereotyper*. Lund: Slavica Lundensia 20.

Train, Kelly Amanda (2000) 'Whiteness, White Otherness and Jewish Identity', *Journal of Mundane Behavior*, 1:2, http://mundanebehavior.org/index.htm (accessed 2004-06-15).

Tulloch, John & Deborah Lupton (2003) *Risk and Everyday Life*. London: Sage.

Tyler, Katharine (2003) 'The Racialised and Classed Constitution of English Village Life'. *Ethnos*, vol. 68:3, 391-412.

'Välfärdsdata, Kronobergs län 2000', http://www.foukronoberg.com/skrifter/vfdata.pdf.

Van Dijk, Teun A. (1987) *Communicating Racism. Ethnic Prejudice in Thought and Talk*. Newbury Park: Sage Publications.

Van Dijk, Teun A. (1993) *Elite Discourse and Racism*. London: Sage.

Waever, Ole & Morten Kelstrup (1993) 'Europe and its nations: political and cultural identities', Ole Waever, Barry Buzan, Morten Kelstrup & Pierre Lemaitre (eds): *Identity, Migration and the New Security Agenda in Europe*. Copenhagen: Centre for Peace and Conflict Research.

Wahl-Jorgensen, Karin (2004) 'A "Legitimate Beef" or "Raw Meat"? Civility, Multiculturalism, and Letters to the Editor', *The Communication Review* 7, 89-105.

Weibull, Lennart (1995) 'Lokal dagstidningsläsning och social skiktning' in Lennart Weibull & Charlotta Kratz (eds): *Tidningsmiljöer. Dagstidningsläsning på 1990-talet*. Göteborg: Institutionen för journalistik och masskommunikation, Göteborgs universitet.

Weibull, Lennart (2000a) 'Förtroendet för dagspressen', Ingela Wadbring & Lennart Weibull (ed.): *Tryckt. 20 kapitel om dagstidningar i början av 2000-talet*. Göteborg: Dagspresskollegiet, JMG, Göteborgs universitet.

Weibull, Lennart (2000b) 'Svenska tidningshus i ett nytt medielandskap', Ingela Wadbring & Lennart Weibull (eds): *Tryckt. 20 kapitel om dagstidningar i början av 2000-talet*. Göteborg: Dagspresskollegiet, JMG, Göteborgs universitet.

Whitebrook, Maureen (2001) *Identity, Narrative and Politics*, London: Routledge.

Wigerfelt, Anders S. (2004) 'Forskning och föreställningar – betydelsen av hur rasism definieras inom forskning och utredningar', Karin Borevi & Per Strömblad (eds): *Kategorisering och integration. Om föreställda identiteter i politik, forskning, media och vardag*. Stockholm: SOU 2004:48.

Wilson II, Clint C. & Félix Gutiérrez (1995) *Race, Multiculturalism, and the Media. From Mass to Class Communication* (2nd ed.). Thousand Oaks: Sage Publications.

Young, Iris Marion (2000) *Inclusion and Democracy.* Oxford: Oxford University Press.

Zaller, John R. (1992) *The Nature and Origins of Mass Opinion.* Cambridge: Cambridge University Press.

Interviewees

Aspman-Walleij, Desk Officer at the Ljungby Job Centre (26 March 2003).

Bengtsson, Carina, (Centre Party), Municipal Commissioner, Municipality of Ljungby (27 March 2003).

Carlsson, ClasGöran, (Social Democratic Party), Municipal Commissioner, Municipality of Ljungby (25 March 2003).

Davidsson, Lars, News Editor, *Smålänningen* (9 April 2003).

Ehn, Siv, project leader, integration programme Dare to Show the Way, Municipality of Ljungby (25 March 2003).

Ekstrand, Roy, Principal of the Vocational High School of Hammarskolan, Ljungby (27 March 2003).

Gustafsson, Christer, Editor-in-chief, *Smålänningen* (9 April 2003).

Idofsson, Sven-Inge, Secretary of the Editorial Board,*Smålänningen* (9 April 2003).

Johansson Janewert (Social Democratic Party), former Municipal Commissioner of the Municipality of Ljungby (9 April 2003).

Johansson, Roland, Chairman of the local political party, The Alternative; deputy of the municipal assembly of Ljungby (26 March 2003).

Lindow, Sixten (Moderate Conservative Party), Former Municipal Commissioner of the Municipality of Ljungby (26 March 2003).

Olsson, Ulf, Head of the Ljungby Job Centre (25 March 2003).

Sjöholm, Leif, Head of Division for Social Issues, Municipality of Ljungby (27 March 2003).

Uvebrant, Villy (Centre Party), Former Municipal Commissioner, Municipality of Ljungby (27 March 2003).

Vong, Jim, Desk Officer for Integration Issues, Board for Social Issues, Municipality of Ljungby (27 March 2003).

Index

About the Author

Bo Petersson (born 1960) is a Professor of Political Science and has been a Senior Lecturer at the Department of Political Science, Lund University since 1996. His special areas of interest include identity constructions, stereotyping, nationalism and xenophobia, and developments in these fields in Europe, Russia, and Central Asia. He has to date written five single-authored books, co-edited four volumes and written approximately 35 articles and book chapters in English or Swedish. His previous major publications in English include *National Self-Images and Regional Identities in Russia* (Ashgate, Aldershot 2001) and Bo Petersson & Eric Clark (eds): *Identity Dynamics and the Construction of Boundaries* (Nordic Academic Press, Lund 2003).

www.ingramcontent.com/pod-product-compliance
Lightning Source LLC
Chambersburg PA
CBHW021820270326
41932CB00007B/269